Gene Long!
Enjoy

A Drunking Problem

Understanding Addiction and Recovery

Richard M. Prodey

NCADD MARYLAND

National Council on Alcoholism and Drug Dependence, Inc. • Maryland Chapter
1202 Maryland Ave. • First Floor • Baltimore, MD 21201 • 410-625-6482 phone • 410-625-6484 fax • www.ncaddmaryland.org

Who is NCADD-Maryland?

The Maryland Chapter of the National Council on Alcoholism and Drug Dependence is a statewide advocacy organization whose mission is to advocate for recovery, treatment, prevention, intervention, and research and to ridding the disease of its stigma and its sufferers from their denial and shame.

What Does NCADD-Maryland Do?

ACCESS TO TREATMENT—Need help finding treatment? Call 410-328-8444 and speak to one of our certified addiction counselors who will try to link people who cannot afford treatment with donated services by providers throughout the state.

DICK PRODEY ADDICTION LECTURE SERIES—Learn about common myths about alcohol and alcoholics, chemical dependency as a disease, the complexity of recovery, attitudes towards addictions and recovery, and the impact of the disease on families. The FREE 8-week series is held every Wednesday from 7:00 to 9:00 p.m. at the Sheppard Pratt Conference Center in Towson. Call 410-296-9747 for directions.

ADDICTION TREATMENT ADVOCATES OF MARYLAND—Discuss ideas and actions related to a range of public policy matters related to addictions and recovery and become part of our legislative action network. This coalition develops and implements an annual legislative agenda targeted at state level activities.

RECOVERY COUNCILS OF MARYLAND—The voices of those in recovery and their family members are desparately needed to ensure smart public policy decisions are made, treatment and recovery support services needs are met, stigma related to the disease is eliminated. NCADD-Maryland is in the process of creating these Recovery Councils.

WWW.NCADDMARYLAND.ORG—Our website has up to date information on key activities and events in Maryland, links to helpful resources, and recommended actions to impact current legislative and budget issues.

CHESS Publications, Inc.

ISBN 0-935273-12-3

Published by CHESS Publications, Inc.
232 East University Parkway
Baltimore, MD 21218

Sponsors

NCADD-MD and CHESS Publications, Inc. wish to thank the following individuals for their generous support toward the publication of this book. Without their help we could not bring this book to press.

In loving memory of our parents,

JOHN AND LOIS WHITE

Susan White Wootton of Atlanta, GA

John D. White, Jr.

W. Daniel White

Robert K. White

Michael A. White, DDS

Dan and Agnes Lafferty

Christopher O'Neil Memorial Fund of the Baltimore Community Foundation

Partners in Recovery

FOREWORD

In the summer of 1980 I was looking for information about alcoholism and drug dependence.

One of my family members was dying from this illness and I started to reach out for help. Each resource I contacted (AA, the Council on Alcoholism, counselors) all said the same thing, "Go to the Dick Prodey Lectures at Sheppard Pratt. You will learn about the disease and recovery." It took about 5 months of hearing about this "lecture series" before I went. But finally I went. And, sure enough, I learned all about alcoholism, drug dependence and recovery. It was a series of eight lectures that covered all of the basics of treatment and recovery but Dick also provided something more. He provided hope; hope for recovery.

The family member could recover and the alcoholic (addict) could recover. It was not only possible, it happened every day. He suggested that we visit some AA meetings and some Alanon meetings to see recovery in person. Recovery became a tangible experience. It happened all the time to all kinds of people.

Dick Prodey is an accomplished teacher and an experieced counselor. He understands this disease from the inside out. He has a rare ability to present the best science in a manner that is accurate and, yet, compassionate. His 25 plus years of experience in the field has been distilled into this book and is presented in a way that family members, recovering people, and professionals can understand it and benefit from it. I highly recommend it to anyone interested in learning more about this disease and recovery.

Robert White
President, NCADD-MD

Dedications

To all the Prodeys I know.

To Mike, Sean, Beth, Brennan and T.C. and to all they love.

To Emma O'Connor Prodey who taught me to respect people and truth equally.

To Pam Prodey whose confidence pushed this project, and whose patience then endured it.

Acknowledgements

Family and friends have suffered through this book's grass roots research. To say I appreciate their understanding is an understatement.

My special thanks to Dr. Penelope Ziegler, Jana Carrington and John Beemer for their recommendations and suggestions.

There are lots of others who have been subjected to my questions about their experiences with addiction and their recovery from it. Their answers were helpful. Always they were hopeful.

TABLE OF CONTENTS

1

ALCOHOL

The earth appears flat. It isn't; it's round. The sun seems to move across the sky from east to west. It doesn't; the earth moves. Plump women were considered beauties during the Renaissance; they modeled nude, their figures admired in great paintings. Today they are too fat for the centerfold. Alcohol appears harmless, a drink. It is a drug.

Perception: Though subtle, there is a significant difference between understanding that alcohol is a drug, and perceiving it as one. For some time it has been known that alcohol is addictive, and yet few people even today think of it as a drug, much less as an addictive one. To us alcohol is a drink. We see it that way because we use it that way, as a beverage. We behave quite differently around alcohol than we do when we are around other drugs. We rarely refer to drunkenness as "overdose." Whiskey is not measured in doses but in shots. When someone is drunk, we hardly ever describe him as drugged. And when we call someone a "drunk," the phrase refers to his character, not the condition of his brain. Alcohol is truth serum, we think, and so we believe that intoxication reveals identity not distorts it, that alcohol releases bizarre behavior, not causes it. The truth, however, is that drugs distort the mind; they do not reveal the truth. Alcohol packs a punch precisely because it is a drug. Someone who is drunk is drugged. Gin irritates brains before it loosens tongues. It also inflames livers.

Alcohol and Overdose: Although Americans are quite familiar with overdoses resulting from alcohol, they rarely associate the word, "overdose," with alcohol. That word is linked to heroin and cocaine use, and not because we are more experienced with heroin or cocaine overdoses. "Overdose" is a drug word, and alcohol is not thought of that way. In general, Americans do not view even extreme drunkenness, with alarm, much less as drug overdose. Nearly everyone over the age of fifteen can tell an Uncle Harry story from first hand experience. At a family gathering Harry slurs his words; his eyes are glazed; he falls back in his chair when he tries to stand, and staggers when he walks. Harry does this because he has had too much to drink. His relatives may be amused, disgusted or disappointed, but few of them are shocked, and fewer still are frightened. Harry is loaded, that's all, and because his condition is alcohol induced, he is taken upstairs to sleep it off while downstairs the party proceeds uninterrupted. No one treats Harry's as a case of overdose because no one perceives Harry as using a drug, not a *real* drug, that is. Had Harry's condition been the result of his taking too many tranquilizers, the party would stop, and Harry rushed to a hospital where relatives would insist his stomach be pumped. They might even want a psychiatrist called for consultation, and might consider involuntary commitment. Those same relatives, however, would not think of taking Harry to a hospital because he was drunk, and if they did, no one would be surprised if told to take him back home. Let Harry swallow pills, and his problem is treated as serious.

Alcohol acts on the brain in a complex way. A simple way of understanding intoxication, however, is to liken it to the brain's falling asleep. Step by step alcohol affects inhibition, judgement, reason, coordination, emotion, muscle control, consciousness, heartbeat and breathing. The word, "intoxication," means literally a poisoned condition. But in America it is barely regarded a drugged condition much less a poisoned one.

In group therapy a young woman described her own progressive intoxication due to Methaqualone. One Quaalude relaxed her. The second made her "free." Those feelings intensified with a third pill, and with succeeding pills she described herself as unable to speak clearly, focus her eyes and walk a straight line. Because her tolerance for the drug was quite high, she did not pass out until a seventh or eighth pill. A middle-aged alcoholic in this same group listened to the description, surprised because it sounded just like getting drunk to him. The man was intelligent. He had been taught that alcohol is a drug, and even claimed to believe that. He just did not *perceive* Vodka as similar to Quaalude, and because he didn't, he failed to see the irony of his insisting that he was an alcoholic and his Quaalude using group member was a drug addict. To his mind they were different.

The Message: In large measure schools have succeeded in educating children about the nature of alcohol. Today sixth graders list correctly its characteristics.

- It is a drug.
- It acts on the brain.
- It is a depressant (long term it's a downer).
- Its action is sedative and hypnotic.
- It is toxic, a poison.
- It is potent.

The school's lessons, however, are quite different from the lessons advertising and the social milieu teaches. And those lessons shape perception:

- Alcohol is fun; drinking is about liberation, friendship and bonding.
- Alcohol is extraordinary (capable of opposites—elation and sedation).
- The rules governing drug use do not apply to alcohol; alcohol is an exception.
- For men drinking is manly. Women who drink, provided they do not get drunk, are liberated.
- Drinking is sophisticated and mature.

The result of such conflicting messages is that children grow up knowing that alcohol is a drug, but failing to perceive it as one. Adults should not be baffled if they fail to relate to alcohol for what it is. As youngsters they were told that alcohol is extraordinary, a beverage they may not drink until they are adults. They are told that it is special, an array of fancy accouterments goes with it. It is harmless; drunks are, after all, funny. It is near magical in its powers; it picks you up as well as calms you down. And alcohol is associated with the strongest motivational forces we know: friendship, sex, love, bonding, wealth, sophistication and power.

None of this is taught. Learning happens without words. The message is subtle and silent, but it is pervasive and persuasive, and it creates not just a way of thinking about alcohol; it fashions a way of *seeing* it. We learn about alcohol's so called "truths" from the places and from the times we set aside for drinking. Alcohol lessons speak to us from billboards, on television, in the movies, on radio and in magazines. We hear the power of alcohol touted in the music we listen to and the literature we read. We absorb lessons about alcohol long before we drink it, unaware of where or when or how we learned what we learned.

Alcohol Places: Consider, for example, what we attach to alcohol from the places we drink it: —in bars, inns and taverns, suggesting camaraderie, fellowship; in night clubs with their bright lights and excitement; and in fancy restaurants. When a society spends lots of money to build places which are used exclusively for a single purpose, that purpose is proclaimed important. We construct bars and elaborately decorate them. The message is unmistakable—so unmistakable that we call the time we spend there "happy hour."

Americans who are distressed by the fact that crack houses are in the middle of their neighborhoods, shocked that drug addicts shoot up in the same block where their children play, fail to appreciate that drug use has been going on at the neighborhood tavern for years.

Alcohol Times: The occasions we claim as drinking occasions also teach us a way to look at alcohol. It is customary to drink at births, at weddings and at deaths. When we come in, and when we go out, someone has a drink. We celebrate life transitions by drinking—at graduations, promotions and retirements. We drink on national holidays, Memorial Day, Labor Day and the Fourth of July. We drink on religious holidays, Christmas. There are even times alcohol is not merely permitted, it is expected. One could argue a case that Americans have a holiday which is, in fact, a drinking holiday—one whose central activity is drinking, and one during which out of control drinking is winked at, if not outright condoned. This holiday is not celebrated on the day it occurs. It is celebrated the evening before. It is called New Year's, but it is not celebrated at the break of dawn of its first day with a ceremony designed to evoke a sense of renewal and hope. It is celebrated the night before, drinking and partying until after midnight—as if it were the ending of the old year and not the beginning of a new one which is celebrated on December's last day. And how do we celebrate the New Year? New Year's is not just celebrated by drinking; it seems reserved for that purpose. Americans in large numbers are expected to drink too much. Coffee stands are set up at roadsides for the occasion. Public service announcements on the media advise us not to avoid drinking but to make coffee the one for the road. January 1st is for football and forgetting—and not just old acquaintances either.

Our tolerance of intoxication is extreme. At what point are we alarmed at how drunk someone is? When he slurs, sees double, staggers, falls down, or passes out? All these are presented in movies as comic. Nearly all are tolerated at significant celebrations. Our notion about what constitutes inappropriate drinking is quite flexible as well, so much so that it is virtually impossible to find circumstances in which alcohol is prohibited without exception. It is clearly not always forbidden on the job; some employees claim they are encouraged to drink with clients. Not everyone who indulges before noon is considered a problem drinker, not if he is a football fan at a tailgate party. Alcohol is not outlawed whenever someone operates heavy machinery, not when the machine is an automobile.

One of the ironic side effects of our society's confusion about what constitutes problem behavior with alcohol is that it helps an already rationalizing alcoholic to delude himself into thinking his drinking falls within the norm. He argues that priests and football fans drink before noon, and so his own morning drinking is not a problem.

Alcohol is Exceptional: A trip to the liquor store should prove how special we consider alcohol. It is packaged in fancy bottles in patriotic (red, white and blue) and in regal (silver and gold) colors. It is called by an array of special names (Miller High Life). It is attractively displayed, and marketed to the whole range of society—from good old boys in overalls to sophisticates in tuxedos. There are dozens of glasses of different sizes and shapes from which to drink alcohol. The sophisticated host soon learns that there are particular glasses for beer, special ones for whiskey, and others in which wine is to be served. Even unsophisticated adults know that a martini is served in a special glass. In fact, there is even a glass with its own name, "Pilsner. "Alcohol must be special if we baptize glasses for its use.

Alcohol's paraphernalia: decanters, stirs, napkins, shakers, strainers, all sorts of accouterments are for sale in uptown and downtown stores. And if the word, "paraphernalia," surprises us, we need to be reminded that alcohol paraphernalia has been a popular collectible in our country a lot longer than coke spoons and pot bongs.

Few Americans would agree to allow a citizen to operate machinery which weighs a ton, has a guidance system responsive to a one inch movement of the hand, develops seven thousands revolutions per minute within seconds, and moves at speeds exceeding sixty miles per hour—while the citizen is drugged. And yet our law permits precisely that, provided that alcohol is the drug and the level of alcohol in the blood stream is "acceptable." Alcohol is exceptional—literally so.

Drinking and Motivation: Among males, beer and bonding go hand in hand. Beer is the complement of hard work, exertion and physical power, according to one ad whose slogan is "It's Miller time." Wine is more a lady's beverage, and is associated with sophisticated sexual encounters. There was even an old television advertisement for a particular wine, which came wrapped in a burlap bag. The ad featured a spokesman in a tuxedo seated at a billiard table, making his pitch, while a woman in a black evening gown stood behind him, silent and motionless. The woman was never spoken to, gestured to or even referred to during the commercial, but an association was communicated.

Whiskey ads stress whiskey's association with prestige, power and position, the clearest example of which were the old "Dewer's Profiles," which highlighted individuals at the top of their professions who drank, of course, Dewers, a brand of scotch. When a sexy woman tells us that Harvey's Bristol Cream Sherry makes it "downright upright" for a woman to invite a man over for a drink, not many of us recognize that the power to break one of society's unwritten laws is being linked to a brand of wine.

The Language of Alcohol: Linguists tell us that language either limits or expands the very thoughts we are capable of having, that, in fact, we cannot have a thought without a word. Language is so potent a means of learning and transmitting perceptions that we must pay particular attention to how we talk about alcohol. When we do, what we find is that our common idioms suggest that alcohol is special and that drinking is fun, but in the common parlance alcohol is rarely called a drug, and only in joking is it proclaimed potent. How seriously are we to take drunkenness when we refer to it as being pickled, looped, sloshed, plastered, bombed, smashed, loaded, wasted, crocked, blitzed, pie-eyed, shit-faced and three sheets to the wind.

At Christmas parties hosts ask guests if they would like "a little something" in their eggnog. Sounds harmless. A glass that needs refilling is "freshened up,"—ironically with a depressant. No bartender would keep his job for long if he asked customers if they preferred their "sedative" shaken or stirred, or if they wanted their "hypnotic" straight up or on the rocks. That well known highball will never be called a Seven and Sedative Hypnotic. Would you like your toxin with a twist?

Despite an American fondness for "telling it like it is," Americans rarely speak of alcohol bluntly, like it is. Alcohol, along with caffeine and nicotine, is legal and socially acceptable, and so it strikes Americans as extreme to speak of those drugs as drugs. It is true that those who use alcohol and caffeine (nicotine has become suspect) infrequently and in limited amounts appear to take limited health risks. Some eight or nine out of ten people who drink alcohol do so without problems. However, as many as 15 percent of our population who start drinking, begin a process which heads in the direction of serious health problems, psychological harm, personal losses, insanity, institutionalization and death. For them alcohol is the agent of a serious disease. It is a drug for everyone.

A Perception Solution: The American perception of alcohol seems wide, deep and immutable, impossible to change. But our perception of a drug can change, and in fact, within the past twenty years Americans have changed their minds about drugs. Marijuana, once regarded as the drug of jazz musicians—exotic and dangerous—has become a recreation for teenagers, and considered relatively harmless by more and more teenagers as well as adults. America *has* changed its perception of marijuana. There is another drug, at one time a very popular one, about which Americans have also changed their minds as well, but this time the change is in the opposite direction. Nicotine within a few years has gone from classy, sophisticated, macho to nasty, smelly—and even addictive. Today smokers are virtually ostracized.

As a society we will appreciate the seriousness of alcoholism as a disease when we come to perceive alcohol as a potent drug. We will find it easier to regard alcoholics as drugged human beings rather than immature ones when we come to see an alcohol soaked brain as a drugged brain. We will begin to recognize that our difficulty with accepting alcoholism as a disease is due, in part, to alcohol's being both so ordinary and so special a part of our culture. We will begin to appreciate how difficult it is for a recovering alcoholic to refrain from alcohol when we appreciate the special role drinking plays in our society. We will deal effectively with the problems arising from alcohol abuse only if we avoid two extreme views - the one, that alcohol is evil, and the other, that it is innocuous.

Unless societal perceptions change, Americans will be faced with the astonishing incongruity that we remain under-insured for the treatment of what we acknowledge to be the number one health problem and number three cause of death in our country.

2

THE "OTHER" DRUGGER

The day of the so called "pure alcoholic," the addict who uses alcohol exclusively, will come to an end if it has not already. Treatment centers, called Alcoholism Programs in the 1980s, are now Chemical Dependency Programs, and the names changed quite simply because the patients had changed. Any alcoholic who is under forty and who has never tried a drug other than alcohol is either lying, been in seclusion, or is in advanced denial. Otherwise he is a dinosaur, a throwback to another era.

Attitudes toward the "other" drugs began changing in the 1960s. By 1990 "recreational" was widely recognized as a term describing both a group of drugs and a way of using them. Attitudes are still changing. Marijuana, which at one time was depicted as the route to "reefer madness," is today considered dangerous only when it is considered a gateway to other drugs. By itself marijuana is thought to be one of the least problematic drugs—and non-addictive, though neither is true. Cocaine's popularity grew steadily in the 1980s, but then the deaths of a popular comedian and a promising college basketball star dealt that drug's reputation a serious blow. By the end of the decade the President of the United States had declared war on it.

Professionals who treat addicts today no longer enjoy the luxury of a simplistic conception in which alcoholics are considered in the mainstream, and other addicts thought to be antisocial, bad or immature. An enlightened view avoids two extremes, that there are no similarities among addicts and that there are no differences among them. Nicotine addicts have something in common with heroin addicts, though the two are not cut from exactly the same cloth.

The Differences: Mood altering drugs differ from each other in several ways. Each produces a pleasurable response as well as unpleasant effects from excessive amounts. Some drugs sedate; they are called downers. Others stimulate and are called uppers. A few create mind movies; these are the hallucinogens. Drugs come in nearly every shape, color, and size. Some are liquid (alcohol); some solid (tranquilizers); and some crystalline (cocaine). Some drugs act quickly; cocaine and heroin produce effects within seconds if injected. Others take longer to "kick in." Some drugs produce serious, even life threatening withdrawal, whereas others produce a withdrawal which is mild enough for one to go to work and function throughout. Some drugs are inexpensive and available twenty-four hours a day seven days a week in every neighborhood of every city and town. Others are available only to those with connections and money.

Though mood-altering drugs differ in several ways, drug addicts differ in just a few:

- Their drug of choice (the drug an addict prefers).
- The extent of other drugs used in addition to the drug of choice.
- The individual's drug use style, i.e., the differences in people, places and paraphernalia surrounding his or her use,
- The legality or illegality of the drug and the means of acquiring it.

Alcoholics and junkies both break the law, and some are caught at it. One generally recognized difference between a heroin addict and an alcoholic is that the alcoholic breaks the law *after* he is loaded, while the heroin addict must break it *before* just to get his supply. Heroin addicts, any addict for that matter whose drug is acquired illegally, is forced to break the law and to justify in his own mind doing so, and for this reason individuals addicted to illegal drugs, if not full-fledged antisocial personalities, tend to have an antisocial streak in them. To the contrary, adult alcoholics acquire alcohol by strictly legal means, and though this does not mean that alcoholics are never antisocial, it does mean that they do not have to do something antisocial just to practice addiction.

As long as certain drugs are illegal and regarded as socially unacceptable, those who gravitate to them will tend to be antisocial. On this point, however, a historical perspective proves quite interesting. The "look" of the typical marijuana user has changed rather dramatically over the last sixty years. The pot smoker of the 1940s seems today quite different from the type who smoked that drug in the 1960s, and the sixties type differs from the 1980s user, who is different yet from those who used the drug in the 90s. By the year 2000, marijuana had become a recreational drug for high school sophomores. If a crystal ball would allow us to see what a typical marijuana addict of the year 2100 might look like if marijuana were legalized today, we might find that look quite different from addicts of today.

The Similarities: Beyond the differences among drugs, addiction to the whole range of drugs is remarkably similar.

- All addiction is progressive.
- Its progression is similar regardless of the drug used.
- Addiction changes personality.
- Tolerance for mood altering drugs develops over time.
- Loss of control is a problem with all mood-altering drugs.

Excellent summaries of drugs, complete with street names, health risks associated with their use, symptoms of dependency, and signs of overdose are available on the internet from government agencies and local police departments. Keeping these volumes current is a never-ending task since drug inventors regularly create new drugs, and users as quickly coin new names. *Ecstasy,* one of the *designer* drugs, so called because it combines two already familiar drugs (Ecstasy combines stimulant and hallucinogenic properties), is an example of drug maker's ingenuity. *Ice,* a name given to a new form of another familiar drug, crystal Methedrine, is another example of both producer's and namer's imaginations.

A Drug and Its Drugger: What health professionals and police departments say about drugs is informative but not nearly as compelling as what addicts say about them. Their line carries special insights because it reveals as much about *other druggers* and their denial as it does about *other* drugs.

Marijuana and Addiction

Marijuana users, for instance, like to believe that pot is not addictive. They consider it safe for two reasons. First, they claim that they suffer no significant problems from its use, and, second, they claim to suffer no profound withdrawal when they stop using. Though it is true that there are pot users who suffer only minimal unpleasant consequences because of the drug, what nearly all marijuana addicts fail to appreciate is how difficult it is for them to quit the drug. Marijuana addiction is subtle. One hardly feels himself a captive of the drug until he tries to quit it. Marijuana addicts ignore too the health consequences, at the very least, the damage to their lungs. They are often blind to the fact that marijuana stands inordinately high in the list of their life priorities.

The one symptom marijuana addicts invariably fail to see as serious is their failure to follow through. Though an individual addict may claim, and correctly so, that he has never committed a crime because of pot, what he overlooks is that he rarely follows through on anything because of it.

The emotional flattening which comes with prolonged use of marijuana is another consequence addicts deny. One psychiatrist with years experience treating addicts refers to it as the *what's the big deal* symptom because chronic pot smokers respond to vital issues with a kind of pervasive emotional flatness. Though their conversation about "head" talk and "head" music can be quite animated, chronic users ask "what's the big deal" about a political election, poverty, nuclear disarmament, war, terrorism and the state of the economy. One young man whose drug of choice was marijuana reported that the only thing different about him since he had started smoking pot was that he "didn't get excited about much any more."

Most significantly marijuana addicts fail to see how their addiction chooses their friends, limits their recreation, dissolves family life, and eventually displaces other interests.

Another curious rationalization for using marijuana is that it is natural, the implication being that what is natural cannot be harmful. Rattlesnakes are natural, but one doesn't play with them.

The myth of the 1960s was that repeated use of marijuana resulted in lowered tolerance so that over time lesser amounts of the drug produced the same or a greater effect, thus making marijuana increasingly economic as well as harmless. It is simply not true. Tolerance for marijuana does develop. Today's smoker inhales a more potent joint than was available to him in the 1960s and thinks his use has not increased, whereas he is simply consuming more THC in fewer *joints*. It is the same mistake an alcoholic makes when he thinks he is drinking less because he has switched from eight bottles of beer to one bottle of whiskey.

According to a pamphlet published by the American Council for Drug Education, sensitive urine tests can remain positive for the constituents of marijuana for as long as two weeks after a single dose. (Blasinsky, p. 6) In treatment centers metabolites of THC in the urine of chronic smokers have been detected for as many as 28 days, and during that time (even after it) individuals are noticeably affected. How individuals are affected varies. Some are agitated; others lethargic. Some admit to feeling distressed; others think not. Nearly all are startled by how long traces of the drug are detectable.

Educators and parents have reason for concern about the counter-educational effects of a single dose of marijuana because of how long it lingers. At the time in their lives when young people need their memories most, pot interferes with memory. Sadly, there are adults for whom abstinence from alcohol and marijuana during adolescence seems extreme. They regard use of a drug as a rite of passage.

Cocaine and Addictability

Cocaine has been around a long time, but addicts are just beginning to teach professionals important lesson about addictability from their experience with that drug. Cocaine confirms the suspicion that drugs with the highest potential for addiction are not necessarily those which produce the quickest and most potent physical dependence. Addictive potential is the measure of how seductive a drug happens to be, and how much craving it provokes. Drugs with the highest potential combine the following characteristics:

- First, drugs produce effects quickly or slowly. For obvious reasons drugs which act quickly have a higher abuse potential than those which act slowly.
- Second, drugs produce either intense euphoric effects or less intense highs. The more pleasurable a drug the more addictable it is.
- Third, a drug's high lasts for a short time or for several hours. When a drug wears off rapidly, the result is twofold: first, the user must dose more frequently to sustain his high; and second, the drug seems more controllable and less harmful.
- Fourth, some drugs generate powerful cravings. Nicotine addicts report craving cigarettes a year or more after they quit. Drugs which produce such cravings must be considered problematic.
- Finally, a drug will be perceived as harmful or harmless. Drugs considered harmless are more appealing than those considered dangerous.

Cocaine has the characteristics mentioned. It is a drug characteristically used in that one-after-another chain of doses which characterizes addiction. Cocaine, in fact, seems more problematic than either heroin or alcohol. Make no mistake, alcohol and heroin are pleasurable, abusable and potentially harmful drugs. But unlike alcohol, cocaine alters one's mood so quickly, especially if injected, and it wears off so rapidly that cocaine packs a double punch. It provides an immediate reward and seems a controllable drug. Also, because cocaine wears off so quickly, users must dose more frequently than with either heroin or alcohol. Finally, unlike alcoholics who prefer their booze with sex, cocaine addicts, some at least, seem to prefer cocaine. Any drug that hits you quick, takes you high and leaves you fast, beckons long after it has been discontinued, and is thought to be safe will invite its user to go at it again and again.

"Crack" is concentrated cocaine, ready to smoke. It has been popular because it packs a punch, is relatively inexpensive, and is easy to hide. But crack's popularity is explained only in part for these reasons. Crack is popular in part because its reputation has been as potent as its punch. A drug's reputation, its newness to the drug use scene, cannot be ignored as one of the factors responsible for its popularity not only among casual users in search of thrills but among seasoned addicts whose tolerance forces them to find newer ways to get high.

PCP, phencyclidine, was popular for a while. Quaalude was too. LSD (Lysergic acid diethylamide) was popular in the 1960s, and in new forms, such as *blotter acid* (LSD dropped on blotter paper) and *Ecstasy,* hallucinogens are making a comeback with a reputation similar to the one they enjoyed in the 1960s. Teenagers are rediscovering the drug of their parent's generation. It should be no surprise that hallucinogens would regain popularity. Horror stories about LSD died. For a variety of reasons teenagers consider hallucinogens harmless, and just as with marijuana, teenagers conclude hallucinogens are safer than other drugs.

Prescription Addiction

The effects of tranquilizers are so much like the effects of alcohol that Valium, Tranxene, Xanax, Serax, Dalmane, Ativan, and Librium, drugs called Benzodiazapines, are referred to as "freeze-dried" alcohol. A recovering Valium addict (it was the only drug this particular patient had ever used) was listening to a group of alcoholics talk about their drinking escapades. Since her addiction had been practiced behind the closed doors of her suburban apartment, she could not identify with barroom antics or the nightclub scene. She could find no parallel between her solitary use and the fellowship drinkers enjoyed. What she could identify, however, was that alcoholics drank for some of the same reasons as she took Valium. She could also discern that the effects of the two drugs were similar enough that she vowed "never to try alcohol," because she was sure she would "like it too much."

The notion that a prescribed drug is less addicting than one available on the street compares in silliness to the assertion that alcohol would be illegal if the government thought it harmful. An addict is an addict whether he is hooked on a prescription drug, on alcohol which is legal and socially acceptable, or on "street" drugs. Mood altering "medicine" makes one as dependent as booze or "junk."

One of the differences between alcoholics, junkies and prescription addicts, however, is that prescription addicts do not like thinking of themselves as *addicts*. Denial deludes them into believing that, even though they may have lots of trouble stopping the drug, they are not addicted to it. Their denial is supported by the acceptability of their drug and the legal means by which they get it. It appears condoned by the medical profession. They reason that they are not drug addicts since a doctor initiated their taking drugs. How could anything be wrong with it? And when they need a doctor's help to withdraw from the drug, they consider that a medical problem, not an addiction.

A prescription addict may sustain his addiction for fifteen years and never once break the law to get his drug. Nevertheless, just as with every other addict, prescription addicts must pursue their drug, and over time that pursuit intensifies. "Scripts" are not pedaled door to door. Doctors do not make house calls surveying which patients need refills. Prescription addicts must seek out and sometimes con their physicians into prescribing.

Denial also keeps prescription addicts from seeing they love their drugs. That love may be neither conscious nor desired. A prescription addict may resent his dependence on the drug, even hate it. He may concede he needs his drug, but he does not like to think he loves it. But he does love it. He loves its effect. He loves the way it makes him feel, and he pursues that just like any other addict. Prescription addicts are not unlike the rejected lover who has been abused repeatedly, but who continues to pursue the abusive relationship. When a prescription addict concedes this, he is usually more embarrassed than street addicts or alcoholics both of whom more readily admit they love the stuff. At its core the prescription addict's denial keeps him holding firm to the belief that he is the victim of his condition and not active in its pursuit.

Addictive Potential: Any drug is capable of being abused, even blood pressure pills. Few people abuse antihypertensives, however. Reducing one's systolic and diastolic may be life saving, but it isn't a whole lot of fun. For a drug to have significant abuse potential it must be one which causes pleasure either because it excites, stimulates, relaxes or relieves. This is generally true. However, even drugs which are regarded as having a very high abuse potential, such as Percodan, cocaine, Xanax or Fiorinal, are not pursued by people who respond to low doses of those drugs in unpleasant ways. Conversely, drugs regarded as having a low potential for abuse have quite a high potential in the hands of the right abuser. Diuretics eliminate fluid from the body and are not a favorite among seasoned addicts (urinating may be a relief, but it is hardly a thrill). In the hands of an anorexic or bulimic or high school wrestler trying to make weight, however, diuretics have seductive power. They are abusable.

Where is the addictive potential? Is it in the drug or the drugger? Only as long as withdrawal-producing physical dependence is considered the exclusive criteria for addiction will we consider potential for addiction a matter of the properties of chemicals. Addiction actually develops not just because drugs have power but because people are attracted to that power. When we realize this, we will grasp addictive potential as involving both the susceptibilities of users and the seductiveness of drugs.

Future research will some day confirm that addiction comes about only when the right drug meets the right drugger. Addiction-ologists know already that, though certain drugs are capable of causing dependence in anyone who abuses them, addiction, in fact, does not befall everyone who uses such drugs. Valium has an accepted reputation for addiction and physical dependence. An elderly woman whose doctor put her on Valium during a period of emotional stress, during which she wrenched her back picking up a heavy load of laundry, took two pills from a bottle of thirty and stopped. She never took a third. Valium made her groggy; she didn't like it. Her reaction to an addictive drug teaches us something about where we are likely to find the potential for addiction. It is as much in people as in drugs.

Most laymen have little trouble acknowledging that an identical dose of aspirin will affect three people differently. One person takes two aspirins and gets relief within half an hour. A second must take three or more aspirins every several hours to get the same relief, and a third finds aspirin irritates his stomach so much he refuses to take more than a single aspirin. Antibiotics affect individuals differently. Penicillin works wonders for one person but makes another sick because he is allergic to it. Why should we have trouble accepting that what is true of aspirin, Lithium, and penicillin is also going to be true of gin, Librium, and nicotine?

3

The Personality of Addiction

Examine these dots.

Connect the dots by drawing four straight lines without lifting the pencil from the paper. Try several times.

This game is frustrating, but not because it is impossible, nor because the instructions are a trick. It is frustrating because one perceives the dots in a way that makes connecting them with four lines impossible. As long as the dots are seen as forming a "box," and as long as one insists on staying within the boundaries of that "box," the problem is unsolvable. The dots are not the problem. It is one's perception of the dots which is the problem. The puzzle is easily solved, but only if one changes his way of *seeing* it.

Perceptions of Alcoholism: Alcoholism perplexes us because our ideas about it are based on perceptions which are inaccurate, misleading, or just plain untrue.

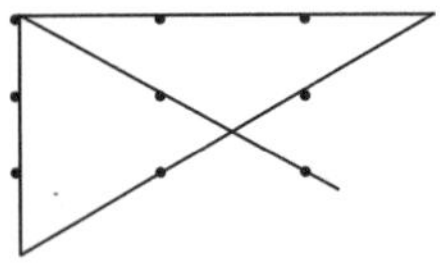

For instance, if we interpret the behavior of an alcoholic based on the notion that alcohol is truth serum, we are likely to draw conclusions about his personality which might be far from the truth. And then if erroneous ideas about alcoholics form the basis for our ideas about alcoholism, a pair of perceptions misleads us. "Alcoholic personality" is a phrase that has been around for so long that people believe that an individual becomes an alcoholic because of his personality. Despite evidence to the contrary, and despite simple common observation of the variety of types of people who become alcoholic, the belief still persists that an anti-social, arrogant, compulsive, dependent, egotistical, depressed, inadequate, irresponsible, or thrill-seeking person is at risk to develop a drinking problem because of those characteristics. Addicts can be dismissed as foolhardy, anti-social, risk-takers if one never actually meets people who are addicted. It is easy to be misled if one ignores the variety of adult addicts and forgets that many of them got started using drugs at a time when university professors were telling them to "tune in, turn on, and drop out," and that the experience was an exploration of reality, not an escape from it.

Just a generation or two ago, law-abiding citizens broke federal law making "bath tub gin" and weren't considered anti-social because of it. Today, Americans are outraged by even the suggestion that drugs be legalized, overlooking one ironic fact. Except during Prohibition, alcohol, the most toxic of the mood altering drugs, has been legal since the country's founding.

If America fails to solve its national problem with drug abuse, it will not be because of overwhelming numbers and insufficient funding alone. It will not be a matter of inadequate health insurance. It will not be a case of too many pushers and too few police. Approaches based on inaccurate perceptions about basics like alcohol and alcoholics and addicts are bound to fail.

Myths about Addicts: Myths are particularly good at muddling the truth because myths are fictions which are nevertheless deeply believed, and myths form the basis of a good deal of what we think about addiction. The myths abound. A short list reveals some old hangers on and a few new twists on old themes. All are untrue.

- Alcoholics drink a lot. To become an alcoholic one must drink heavily.
- "Hard" stuff is the risky form of alcohol. Risk is reduced if one sticks to beer and wine. Mild drugs, such as marijuana, are not addictive.
- People who are dependent on prescription drugs are not real drug addicts. They are just following doctor's orders.
- Alcoholics and drug addicts cannot go very long without drinking and drugging.
- The classic alcoholic is the skid row bum, and the real drug addict injects hard drugs.
- All true addicts inject drugs.
- Morning drinking is hard-core. One who limits his drinking to evenings has no problem.
- Sixteen is too young to be alcoholic.
- Sixty is too old to be a drug addict.
- Real alcoholics drink in binges.
- Addicts mix drugs. Stick to one drug and you're safe.
- Addicts use drugs as a form of protest against society. They act out.
- Alcoholics choose alcohol over the important things in life; they are irresponsible.
- Primary alcoholism is a male problem. Alcoholic women have psychiatric problems.
- Alcoholics are egotists. They put their own pleasure before anyone or anything else.
- Drug addicts go through a phase, which they either outgrow or get hooked.
- One is not addicted until he gets the "shakes."
- Alcohol is truth serum; it reveals personality.
- For the most part, drinking is an escape from reality.
- Teenagers who smoke marijuana are self-medicating an underlying depression.

Definitions of Alcoholism: Very few people bother to write out their personal, formal definition of alcoholism, and yet most people do have a working definition of it. These definitions are formed from the mental pictures we have of alcoholics and addicts, and often those images come from movies. The problem is that movies depict addicts in extreme ways. It sells tickets.

There are formal definitions of alcoholism, and those definitions represent a variety of ways of thinking. Consensus among the experts is hard to come by. But if a single definition were created from only those elements common to all of the expert definitions, what would that composite be, and how would the popular mythology of alcoholism stack up against it? The following are the expert definitions. With one exception they are listed from oldest to most recent.

> "any use of alcoholic beverages that causes any damage to the individual or society or both." (Jellinek, p. 35)

> "...an illness, characterized by preoccupation with alcohol and loss of control over its consumption which usually leads to intoxication if drinking is begun; by chronicity; by progression; and by tendency toward relapse. It is typically associated with physical disability and impaired emotional, occupational, and/or social adjustments as a direct consequence of persistent and excessive use of alcohol." (American Medical Association, p. 6)

> "...includes three criteria all of which must be present for the person to be regarded as an alcoholic: (a) Large quantity of alcohol consumed over a period of years; (b) Abnormal, chronic loss of control over drinking, shown by inability to refrain or inability to stop; and (c) The drinking causes chronic damage to physical health or social standing." (Barry and Walgren, pp. 716-717)

> "Includes a condition in which alcohol is consumed to the detriment of a person's health or social functioning over a period of time." (Edwards et. al., p. 41)

> "Alcoholism is a chronic, progressive, and potentially fatal disease. It is characterized by tolerance and physical dependency

or pathologic organ changes, or both—all the direct or indirect consequences of the alcohol ingested. The person with alcoholism cannot consistently predict on any drinking occasion the duration of the episode or the quantity that will be consumed." (National Council on Alcoholism, p. 764)

"...any use (of alcohol) that interferes recurringly with the person's health, job, or society, including family." (Whitfield, p. 7)

"a chronic, primary, hereditary disease which progresses from an early physiological susceptibility into an addiction characterized by tolerance changes, physiological dependence, and loss of control over drinking. Psychological symptoms are secondary to the physiological disease and not relevant to its onset." (Milam, p. 170)

"a chronic disease, or a symptom of an underlying psychic or physical disorder, characterized by dependence on alcohol for relief from psychic or physical distress or for gratification from intoxication itself, and characterized by a consumption of alcoholic beverages sufficient and consistent enough to cause physical or mental or social or economic disability. The dependence is manifested by loss or impairment of control over drinking." (Keller, p. 20)

"Alcoholism becomes a disease when loss of voluntary control over alcohol consumption becomes a necessary and sufficient cause for much of an individual's social, psychological, and physical morbidity." (Vaillant, p. 44)

"Alcoholism is a primary, chronic disease with genetic, psychosocial and environmental factors influencing its development and manifestations. The disease is often progressive and fatal. It is characterized by continuous or periodic impaired control over drinking, preoccupation with the drug alcohol, use of alcohol despite adverse consequences and distortions in thinking, most notably denial." (American Society of Addiction Medicine and the National Council on Alcoholism and Drug Dependence, Inc., p. 1.)

Interestingly, Alcoholics Anonymous never defines alcoholism. What comes closest to a definition is AA's first step of The Twelve Steps.

> "We admitted we were powerless over alcohol; that our lives had become unmanageable." (Alcoholics Anonymous, p. 59)

How does popular myth compare to these studied formulations? One of the most common myths is that alcoholics drink the "hard stuff" and lots of it. Yet only one of the above definitions mentions heavy drinking, and not a single one mentions that a particular type of alcohol is necessary to becoming an alcoholic. Morning drinking, according to myth, is what makes an alcoholic, even though the experts are silent on the point. Alcoholics are supposed to love to drink and love being drunk. They are believed to have been drinkers for many years. The experts, however, do not echo any such sentiments. Many laymen believe that physical dependence is the distinctive criteria of drug addiction, but the experts do not share that opinion. More than a few people believe that personality or family rearing causes alcoholism. The experts do not concur.

Nearly every one of the expert definitions does contain the seeds of the notion of "loss of control," but that phrase is not defined clearly enough in each instance to determine whether the experts agree on it. One alcoholism thinker uses "primary loss (or impairment) of control" to mean the inability to refrain from a first drink in a drinking episode, and "secondary loss (or impairment) of control" to signify the inability to stop once started (Keller, p. 162). Thirty years earlier Dr. Jellinek used the same phrase to mean an alcoholic's progressive inability to control the amount he or she drinks once he begins (Jellinek, 1960). And it is the latter notion which the National Council echoes in its 1976 definition when it says the person with alcoholism "cannot consistently predict on any drinking occasion the duration of the episode or the quantity that will be consumed." Throughout this book *loss of control* is used to mean that phenomenon in which an initial dose of drug sets off a chain of doses which ends in acute intoxication. Early on, alcoholics *lose control* once in a while. In time, that problem worsens, and by the end, it becomes a consistent pattern. The experts, however, are unclear about whether they agree.

The experts do agree on two points. Alcoholics drink. Their drinking causes problems. What emerges as a synthesis of their definitions, once the differences are removed, is essentially what members of Alcoholics Anonymous have said for years. It is not what you drink, how much, how often, where, when, or even why you drink, but what happens as a result of drinking which determines whether you are alcoholic.

A boiled-down, descriptive definition of alcoholism is as simple as this. Alcoholism is drinking which causes recurring, significant life problems. "Recurring" is an important modifier because it seems premature to label someone "alcoholic" if his drinking has caused only a single problem. "Significant" is also an important modifier because most people are unwilling to label someone as alcoholic even if he had recurring hiccups due to drinking.

The definition is descriptive not etiological. It presents a picture of a condition once the condition has occurred without proposing to explain why the condition comes to be. Adhering to a common sense principle which holds that something ought not be called a problem until it *is* one, this definition suggests that an individual is not called "alcoholic" until drinking causes problems. It sidesteps the issue of whether he is born alcoholic without excluding the possibility that he or she may, at birth, be prone to handle alcohol in a way which could lead to problems later in life.

What is an alcoholic? An alcoholic is a person with alcoholism. Though admittedly circular, the statement is no more ridiculous than calling a diabetic someone with diabetes. An alcoholic is not a type of personality. He is a person with a type of disease. "Alcoholic" is simply an adjective, the one which refers to a person with a particular disease, alcoholism.

Is there, then, an alcoholic or an addictive personality? Research has answered the question. Dr. Vaillant, in *The Natural History of Alcoholism,* summarizes a longitudinal study of several decades by concluding that the so-called "alcoholic personality" is not the cause of alcoholism but the result of it (Vaillant, p. 312). Anyone who has hung around recovering alcoholics long enough to get past first impressions soon realizes the truth of it. As a group, what alcoholics share is not a similar personality, but a similar impact on personality from a similar experience, alcoholism.

Before Alcoholism: Alcoholics report their personalities before alcoholism were as diverse as any found among members of the human race. Some alcoholics enjoyed well-adjusted, adult success before they started drinking, whereas others suffered from serious psychiatric disorders. A portion of those who later became alcoholic had personality problems severe enough to cause difficulty early in life. Some were angry youngsters; others were compliant, and a few were model teenagers. Many an alcoholic appears to have had little more than the common problems of adolescence, but those typical problems never had the chance to be typically resolved. Instead alcoholism entered their lives, and, as a result, maturity didn't. A significant percentage of alcoholics are the products of homes headed by an alcoholic parent and consequently had problems before getting sick with their own addictions. Some were normal in every way. Six kinds of people become chemically dependent, each with his or her own problems beforehand.

- Normal people with life's usual share of difficulties;
- Those for whom addiction started early, cutting short important developmental stages;
- Children of alcoholics for whom dysfunctional family life created problems;
- Youngsters whose childhoods were marked by physical, emotional and / or sexual abuse;
- Character disordered individuals whose personality problems preceded addiction, and
- Those with primary psychiatric disorders, such as schizophrenia, depression, or bi-polar disorder.

But chemical dependency, regardless of which drug is used, is a personality changing experience. Varied personalities may enter the process, but personality is subjected to such similar shaping forces that the phrase, "personality of addiction," does a better job of capturing the relationship of addiction to personality than "addictive personality," which suggests a predictive or causative condition.

An addict who had psychological problems before becoming addicted is sure to be worse off after, but even normal people change after a few years. To be subjected to the forces of addiction for twenty years warps personality. What emerges from the bottle ranges not from good to bad but from bad to worse.

Personality Changing Factors: It is little wonder that addicts end up described as

- depressed,
- anti-social,
- mistrustful, suspicious, paranoid,
- whose emotional lives are restricted,
- who find intimacy difficult,
- who have trouble sustaining relationships,
- who have big egos,
- who are overly sensitive,
- emotionally labile,
- defensive,
- with low self esteem

Over years addiction changes people. No single factor produces those changes. At least four powerful forces are at work producing such changes:

- a potent drug acts on the brain;
- the mind is distorted by denial and rationalization;
- emotions are distorted, dulled and exaggerated;
- the whole process wrecks one's spirit.

The Impact on the Brain: By definition, mind altering drugs affect the mind. They do so in part because they alter the brain. Though each drug has effects characteristic of it, all mood-altering drugs act on arousal centers of the brain producing alternating states of sedation and irritation. Though in a different sequence, depressants and stimulants both make the brain go "up" and "down." Even heavy smokers are familiar with nicotine's cycles of stimulation, lethargy and irritation. Quite simply, a drug acts on a brain, and that changes personality.

Life Chemically Filtered

Addicts function on a regular, sometimes daily basis, in one of three chemically altered states: chemically elated, sedated or agitated. To think that someone so regularly altered would remain unchanged is akin to claiming that a patient prepped for surgery with sedative drugs every day for several weeks would be unaffected by the experience. An addict processes life and life experiences through a brain which is chemically affected. The incoming data itself is altered.

Memory Problems

Abusive drug use causes memory problems, and even when such problems are not permanent, a life of forgetting leaves its mark. Non-addicts know how embarrassing it is to forget the birthday of a good friend. For alcoholics the impact can be gauged by multiplying one forgetting by years of forgetting, and then adding memory blackouts.

Toxic Experience

Some alcoholics do their thinking so regularly drugged that they consider it normal. In alcoholism's final stage, alcoholics get to join that special group of people who experience the bizarre, the psychotic, the terrifying. Fears, strange and sudden, visit them. Brains that are poisoned fashion personalities that are poisoned.

The Impact on the Mind: Addiction affects the mind as well as the brain. This happens in several ways, withdrawal the most dramatic. Anyone who has suffered through acute withdrawal—been delusional, felt his heart palpitate, convulsed, shook uncontrollably, hallucinated or suffered delirium tremens does not soon forget the experience. It is unforgettable. But addiction affects the mind in subtler ways.

Fear of Recurrence and Shame

Long after a withdrawal hallucination has ended, the sufferer harbors concerns about his sanity, fearing he will hallucinate again. For most of her hospital treatment an elderly woman refused to admit she had hallucinated that water was pouring through the walls of her room because she feared that such an admission would prove her insane and prolong her stay. A middle aged truck driver, hospitalized after he claimed to have seen "little black men climbing in his Christmas tree," was struggling six months later, trying to accept the experience as normal for an alcoholic in severe withdrawal. It was more than six months before he was confident he would not hallucinate again. Another patient discharged a pistol at a band of Indians he believed had invaded his living room. He confessed to killing one of them the day he was admitted to the hospital. Later, he refused to talk about the experience as much out of embarrassment as fear. It wasn't until a year later that he could laugh about it.

A Mind Shaped by Denial

For a variety of reasons alcoholics have shameful, silly, bizarre, perverted, frightening, even psychotic experiences, but in order to persist in drinking they must deny that those experiences are caused by alcohol. Denial will not permit an active alcoholic to blame alcohol, and so he must find someone or something else to blame. And so he blames his own mind. More than a handful of alcoholics prefer a psychiatric diagnosis as the way to account for their behavior rather than believe that the drugs they love make them crazy. Alcoholics spend a lifetime analyzing their personalities, an analysis based on data which they have gathered about a drug-poisoned subject, and then they believe the analysis to be true because the alternative is unacceptable.

The Effect of Rationalization

Growing tolerance plays a role in changing personality. Tolerance forces an alcoholic to find reasons for why he drinks more and more often. Sometimes he blames others for it. A wife, a lover, a Pope, a President, an evil boss, the Western system, inheritance of a melancholic disposition, an unfortunate childhood, inadequate educational opportunities, too many dependent children, a stressful job, even a wicked step-mother have been blamed for causing alcoholics to drink. Rationalizing changes minds, and it changes lives, turning friends who confront into enemies. Rationalizing chooses one's friends, ends relationships, quits jobs, and alienates friends. It creates a patchwork of distortions, which very likely accounts for the isolation and loneliness alcoholics end up with.

Prescription addicts must rationalize too. They must convince themselves that the pain for which they were given a prescription has gotten much worse in order to justify taking more and more potent painkillers. They even invent pain in order to justify needing medication. Ironically, more than a few who have become hooked on prescription drugs started out with legitimate prescriptions for real health problems, but the drugs which originally relieved pain eventually made it worse. Addiction is a trap. Justifying it is another kind of trap.

Projection and Its Effect

Projection is that trick of mind by which an individual sees in others what he is unhappy with and rejects in himself. It, too, impacts personality. If I believe that drinking is an angry activity in our society when it is really my own angry drinking which is unacceptable to me, that projection will affect me in far-reaching ways. I may end up constructing a philosophy which claims the world is an angry place, believing that my thoughts are based on truths "out there" when actually their source is in me. And when the world becomes an angry place, it becomes a frightening place too. The denial, rationalizations, distortions, manipulations and exaggerations needed to sustain even an ordinary addiction, if they have enough time to work on a personality, are capable themselves of creating the character disorders described in *The Diagnostic Manual.* One need not have a personality disorder at the start of alcoholism to end up with one.

Projection of Self-Mistrust

Addiction is hiding. Even before an alcoholic sneaks a drink, he hides how much he drinks; he hides its consequences; he hides his feelings about it, and he hides the effect it has at home. If others were to see his pain and his shame, his loneliness and his fear, even he would have to admit that something is wrong, and so he hides his feelings. When he is asked how he feels, he answers that he is fine even though at that very moment he may be contemplating suicide. *What you see is not who he is,* and such duplicity, a calm exterior hiding a turbulent soul, persuades the alcoholic that he is fake, a phony. If he then projects this onto others, he begins believing that everyone fakes it—that no one can be trusted. When addicts hide behind smiles, they find it difficult not to believe that all smiles are masks, and all caring pretense. They learn to mistrust.

Shattered Ego Boundaries

One feature of the personality which addiction fashions convinces family members that alcoholics have deep emotional problems. It is common for addicts to swing between grandiosity and self-abasement, from arrogance one moment to self-doubt the next, from egotistical to insecure. The mental health professional who is unfamiliar with how common this is may well interpret ego vacillations and shaky ego boundaries as indicating a borderline personality, a disorder that can be quite severe. There are alcoholics who are Borderline Personalities, of course, but ego extremes come built into even garden-variety cases.

Bloated, shaky egos are common among alcoholics, and the reason is quite evident when one looks at what happens to a drinker's ego during a bout of drunkenness. Anyone with the capacity to drink beyond normal limits without passing out has the opportunity to witness his ego surpass normal limits. On a single night of uncontrolled drinking, an alcoholic witnesses his ego fly off in extreme directions: from extremely inflated to extremely deflated. At 9:00 p.m. with a rising blood alcohol level, he sees himself as handsome, wise, strong, witty, powerful, charming, brilliant, insightful and full of genius. By 2:00 a.m. the same fellow who, a few hours earlier, was finding solutions to world problems now has trouble finding a bathroom to be sick in. The grandeur and humiliation of a single night of such extremes, multiplied by many nights over many years, creates what AA members call "an egotist with an inferiority complex." After a dozen years of such bloat and shrink, an alcoholic ends up feeling alternately powerful and useless, simultaneously brilliant, shy and uncertain. Chemical dependency shatters many boundaries. Extreme behavior is common. Ego extremes are run of the mill.

It is axiomatic of chemical dependency that when one see the arrogant side of an alcoholic, one can assume that beneath lies shaken confidence and shattered self esteem. Conversely, behind a self-abasing exterior often lurks an ego, grand and powerful. Addiction teaches peaks and pits.

The Impact on Feelings: Addiction wreaks havoc on emotional life. Because alcoholics learn about their feelings under the influence of drugs, they come to believe that feelings are intense, numbed, exaggerated and agitated, but hardly ever normal. Six beers turn sadness into depression. A pint of bourbon pushes depression to despair and despair to suicidal thinking. Fueled by martinis, anger erupts as rage. Anxiety turns to terror. And it is not just unpleasant feelings that seem out of control; even pleasant ones seem that way. Drunken love comes out as lust, dripping sentimentality or undying loyalty for strangers. It is as outlandish as drunken anger. Alcoholics either do not feel, or they feel out of control, and so feelings come to be embarrassing and frightening. Feeling itself is mistrusted.

Alcoholics also have difficulty in what ought to be the simple matter of naming their feelings. One recovering woman with more than usual difficulty recognizing when she was angry realized that she had equated *real* anger with what she felt when drunk. One night in a drunken rage she shattered a glass shower door with the back of her hand. After that, subsequent anger seemed no match for the memory of glass and blood splattered over bathroom walls. Eventually alcoholics learn to be afraid not only to express feelings, but also to have them. Experience teaches them that to feel is to feel out of control.

Sudden Feelings

Chemical dependency not only appears to alter moods, it manufactures them. Even in its early stages, chemical dependency generates sudden feelings and changes in feeling states. The following experiences are common even among young addicts. An evening of drinking begins in good humor and ends in tearful self-pity. Intense anger flares out of someone who a minute before was joking. A celebration devolves into melancholy. Unpredictability of this sort makes abnormal drinkers wonder what secrets lie hidden in them, creating all sorts of confusing data to be analyzed the next day—hung over.

A Shame Structured Personality

In addition to the confusion which sudden feelings create, more subtle problems develop over years—guilt and shame the most significant of these. In the thick of addiction an alcoholic feels vaguely uncomfortable about his drinking. As time passes, he feels guilty about neglecting others. Later, he comes to be ashamed of not measuring up to his own expectations as well as the expectations of others. As his disease progresses, he suffers unbearable remorse about drunken behavior which can be as bizarre, strange, foolish, cruel and perverted as behavior ever has been.

Guilt and shame are insidious; they begin playing roles long before an alcoholic is "falling down" drunk. One story illustrates the point and is memorable not just because it should have happened only in the movies, but because it illustrates how *loss of control* affects an alcoholic even before he or others realize he has a drinking problem. A handsome and distinguished man had already developed a problem controlling his drinking at a time in his life when he drank infrequently. On one such occasion, at a party in his freshman year of college, alcohol had gotten the better of him before he knew it. At the party there was a stunning young woman this gentleman drinker wanted to impress. He engaged her in conversation and maneuvered her off to the side of a room near a window through which a cool, late summer breeze was blowing. He felt sparkling, debonair and completely impressive, but he was already drunker than he thought. With a drink in one hand, he crossed his feet at the ankles and lifted his other hand to lean casually against the wall. He was, however, standing next to an open window. He left the party sooner than intended. After he picked himself out of the bushes, he returned to his dorm, and for the rest of his college career went to great lengths to avoid being seen by the young woman he so wanted to impress. He never dated her. He never had the relationship he had hoped for. Drinking affected more than his dignity. Alcoholism affected him thirty years before he entered treatment for it. Addiction fashions a personality structured around shameful experiences.

"Next Day Guilt"

An alcoholic is ashamed of drunken behavior. He is ashamed of next day behavior as well. But because he cannot excuse himself the next day by claiming he was drunk, he holds himself fully accountable for it, sometimes harshly so. Addicts begin believing they are just plain mean or bad. What they almost always fail to take into account, of course, is that even though they are not drunk the next day, they are still drug-affected; the alcohol which sedates them Friday night agitates them nearly all of Saturday. Alcoholics are *under the influence* not for just those hours when booze is in the blood stream. They are under its influence, in some cases, for days later. Guilt about the "next day" takes years to overcome.

Fear

Addiction serves up extra helpings of fear. Alcoholics fear they will be found out. They are afraid of what they might have said or done during blackouts. Fear turns to paranoia, a paranoia which results from an overblown, overly sensitized ego, from hiding, from fear of exposure, and, of course, from the drug itself. Marijuana makes some of its smokers paranoid. Alcohol makes alcoholics paranoid, and stimulant abusers report feeling intensely suspicious under the influence of those kinds of drugs. But an addict's fears do not start out as full-blown paranoia. At first, he worries he will be discovered as a fraud, that others will see his surface confidence as a sham, that his facade will collapse to expose him as cruel to those he is supposed to love. Eventually he fears drinking will destroy him, but long before that, other fears are at work. The insidiousness of chemical dependency is that it distorts emotional life so early in the process that drinkers fail to connect their emotional problems to growing alcoholism. Instead they ascribe those problems to personality.

The Loneliness of Addiction

Eventually alcoholic drinking completely isolates an alcoholic. He is lonely because he cannot share his feeling, and he cannot share them, in part, because he is ashamed of them. Addiction breeds loneliness.

A Spiritual Disease: "Spiritual illness" is a difficult concept. A good many people have a tough time accepting such an idea. Human beings already have enough ways of being sick without inventing new ones, for sure. But, alcoholism does affect the spirit, and a phrase such as "spiritual illness" might well shed a special light on addiction in two ways: it gives a name to the despair addicts feel, and it points toward a path of recovery.

An alcoholic's body must heal. His brain must heal. But his spirit must heal too. Whatever solution one finds for addiction, that solution must be powerful enough to dissolve years of shame. It must help one reconcile the terrible sense that he has wasted his life. It must fill the void when recovery takes away from him what has provided structure and meaning and freedom and fun. It must reverse cynicism. It must heal resentfulness.

Addiction's damage is total. It destroys faith. "Prove it" becomes the addict's attitude. It diminishes hope - hope that he can recover, hope that his family will trust him ever again. Addiction renders one unloved and unloving, unfit to give love, unworthy to receive it. It creates despair even in those who seem to have all the things which make life hopeful—job, home, loved ones. Relapse after relapse deadens the spirit. Skid row renders in visible terms what happens inside to many.

4

Moral Problem, Symptom, or Disease?

At first, calling alcoholism a disease seems ridiculous, a cop-out. Hard-liners are concerned that if alcoholism is called a "disease," then drug addiction will be called one, and then bad habits will be considered diseases, and finally the word, "disease," will come to mean anything which is wrong with anyone. For sure, it is a crime against language when a word becomes meaningless because it is used to refer to anything or everything. Fear that every ache and pain, simple discomfort, or even the common cold will be classified as diseases, however, should not keep reasonable people from considering alcoholism a "disease" if it fits, if "disease" explains the phenomenon.

The truth is that "disease" does a better job of explaining what happens to people who develop a drinking problem than any of the other names which have been used to describe that process. "Disease" does a better job of explaining the sheer numbers of alcoholics in this country—millions of them—than does the notion that so many people would happen to come up with the same weakness or sinfulness. "Disease" does a better job of shedding light on why so wide a range of personalities develop a drinking problem than the notion that so many different types would have fallen victim to an identical personal failing. "Disease" is more logical than "psychiatric disorder" as a way to explain why many alcoholics recover without professional psychiatric treatment, unless, of course, we are prepared to accept the unlikely possibility that hundreds of thousands of psychiatrically disturbed people with serious psychiatric problems would spontaneously remit.

Some recovering alcoholics consider the controversy over whether alcoholism is disease or misconduct an academic discussion at best. To them what is important is that they have it, regardless of what it is called. Others, however, suffer unnecessarily because they persist in believing what they were taught as children, that an alcoholic is a bum, a wastrel, a misanthrope, that he is a sinner, misguided, incorrigible, spineless, and weak; that he has a dependent, compulsive, incompetent, inadequate, or sociopathic personality. Based on such thinking, they pursue a course aimed at reforming bad habits rather than doing the one thing which might help, namely abstaining from alcohol.

Searching for a Name: In one sense and without meaning to diminish it, the degeneracy versus disease debate is a debate about a name. The issue is as much philosophical as it is medical, and so it is important to consider what we expect a name to do when we use it to label an experience.

We hang a name on a new experience hoping to accomplish two things. First, we hope the name sheds light on what it is attached to by pointing out how it is similar to something which is already familiar to us, so that when others come across the experience they will quickly understand it because of its name. Secondly, we hope the name leaves nothing major unexplained. If we call a room which is the size of a telephone booth a "movie theater," that name leaves unexplained a great deal about the room, especially that only one person at a time can watch a movie in it. The name is useless. Traditionally alcoholism has been labeled a "moral problem," a "symptom of an underlying psychiatric disorder," and a "primary disease." Which does the best job?

Observations about Alcoholism: Most people have limited opportunity to observe alcoholism. A layman's observations are limited to only a few cases, and often those are cases with whom the observer is involved in an emotional way. Little can be learned about alcoholism in general from such observations. On the other hand, if one had the chance to witness thousands of cases, representing a variety of people, from different cultures, in different social settings, and at different periods in human history - if one had the chance to witness the life span of affected individuals and see it from a detached vantage point, several characteristics would emerge. Whatever name we give alcoholism must shed light on a problem which is

- Insidious
- Complex
- Primary
- Chronic
- Progressive
- Treatable

An Insidious Problem: Chemical dependency is insidious; in other words, sneaky. It is sneaky in several ways. Alcoholics consider alcohol a friend, a problem solver not a problem causer. Because they focus on its immediate effect, alcoholics believe alcohol makes them feel good. Except for hangovers, and some do not suffer from severe hangovers, alcoholics fail to connect the unpleasant agitation they feel the following afternoon and evening to alcohol. On Friday he feels good, but the price the alcoholic pays for Friday's pleasure lasts most of the following day, and as dependency grows, part of the next week as well.

Chemical dependency is sneaky in another way. Its damage is not always visible and not always dramatic. Health problems caused by alcohol abuse may go undetected for a long time. Many a functioning alcoholic seems a model parent, an outstanding citizen, and a hard worker. Even astute family members are embarrassed to learn they have been living with an active alcoholic for years without realizing it.

The onset and progression of symptoms is another of addiction's insidious ways. In some cases symptoms develop so gradually that they are imperceptible, and in other cases, symptoms appear so early that they are not seen as "symptoms" at all. For someone whose drinking has been pathological from the start, it takes time to realize there is something unusual about it.

A Complex Problem: Alcoholism is called complex, because it is not a single faceted problem but rather multi-faceted. And each facet—its causes, its effects, and its peripheral results—complex as well. Addiction is a complex of causative factors. It is a problem which gives birth to problems. It is an illness which affects its victims in a variety of ways.

Complex Causes

What causes compulsive drinking and what causes alcoholism are related questions but different ones. Science will some day convince the world that the reason one person is prone to alcohol addiction and another not has to do with biochemical differences between them. In other words, heavy drinking or drug use, adaptation to a drug, sensitivity to the damage a drug does, tolerance for it, or any combination of these factors are matters primarily, if not exclusively, of one's biochemical make-up, not of the personality. And yet it seems simplistic to conceive of addiction which takes years to develop as the result of a single or even a cluster of biochemical factors alone. Alcoholism, when defined as drinking which causes problems, involves multiple forces, just one of which, though a crucial one for sure, is one's biochemical pre-disposition toward compulsive alcohol use.

By itself alcohol no more causes alcoholism than gasoline causes automobile accidents. Alcohol is an ingredient and a necessary one, but the role it plays is analogous to the role a baseball plays in a baseball game. The ball is essential to the game; one cannot play baseball without it, but by itself, without bats, players, bases, umpires and a field, the ball will not cause a baseball game. It will just sit on the pitcher's mound. Alcohol's role in alcoholism is similar.

The making of bread provides an analogy for how multiple factors come together to create something, in alcoholism's case—a problem. Bread is the result of several ingredients: a "magic" ingredient, an ingredient which one might say is "susceptible" to becoming bread, and that ingredient is yeast. Yeast then needs warm water to activate it. Flour, sugar, salt and some other ingredients give each loaf of bread its distinctive "character." Finally, the mixture needs time for rising and an oven for baking. Each of bread's ingredients has an analog in alcoholism.

Yeast and Water—Susceptible Host and Activating Agent

Yeast has the potential to be bread. It might be said to be prone to becoming bread. In alcoholism what is the analog to yeast? Research has yet to identify exactly what factor or factors make one prone to alcoholism, but research from different sources points to the involvement of genetic factors (Bohman, 1978; Bohman et. al., 1981; Cadoret, 1980; Goodwin, 1976 and 1979; Goodwin et. al., 1973; Goodwin et. al., 1974; Schuckit, 1980; Schuckit & Goodwin, 1972; Schuckit & Rayses, 1979). Some research even suggests that the reason one person may be susceptible to stimulant drugs and another to depressants is because of mechanisms under neurogenetic not psychological control (Cloninger, 1987). Adaptation, tolerance, and *loss of control* so characteristic of alcoholic drinking may be the products of genetic factors (Milam, p. 32). In other words, research suggests not that alcoholism is inherited but that susceptibility to it may be passed on genetically.

Actually, one does not have to have read detailed research to believe that susceptibility to mood altering drugs, such as alcohol, is a biochemical matter. Concerning other drugs most people accept readily that in any group of people there is likely to be a percentage who will respond to a particular drug in a troublesome way. Aspirin, for example, provides quick and effective relief for some, while others need double doses to get aspirin's relief, and some find that aspirin so irritates their stomachs they rarely ever use aspirin. Penicillin works wonders for most, but some people get sick from it. Like aspirin and penicillin, alcohol is a drug. And so, what is true for one drug, like Ibuprofen, is likely to prove true for another, like gin. Quite simply, there will always be people who are resistant to the effects of a drug as well as those who are susceptible to having problems because of it, along with those for whom the drug is effective and safe.

Claiming that genetic factors are involved in developing a drinking problem is not to say that everyone who has an alcoholic parent is doomed to become an alcoholic. What it says is that alcoholism is a disease which involves a "susceptible host," one in whom a kind of yeast waits to be activated. But before yeast becomes bread, it must meet water. Water kicks off yeast's potential; it is an activating "agent." Alcoholism's agent is alcohol, an activator and stimulator which starts a process and nourishes it along. When defined as drinking which causes problems, alcoholism is impossible without alcohol. Infants are not born divorced, fired from jobs, or charged with driving while intoxicated. An infant may be born susceptible to alcohol, a potential alcoholic, but if he never drinks, he will never know.

Character Factors

Yeast and water alone are not bread. Other ingredients must be added—flour, sugar and those ingredients which give each loaf of bread its own texture, substance and flavor, its own distinctive character so to speak. In chemical dependency, the ingredients are personality and character which play an analogous role. Psychological factors do play a role in alcoholism, but those factors, are not always abnormal factors. In fact, any force which supplies a susceptible drinker a reason to drink plays a role in feeding his susceptibility if he has it. It is to be expected, therefore, that the behavioral factors involved in a developing addiction will differ with individuals. One person's reason for drinking may be as innocent as his belief that alcohol is the way to celebrate, and he celebrates regularly. Someone whose life is stressful and who turns to alcohol in times of stress, will find stress playing a role in his developing an addiction, provided he is susceptible to the drug he uses. A thrill seeker will be at greater risk than someone who is temperamentally conservative, if, of course, the thrill seeker is susceptible to drugs. Someone with an anxiety disorder will find anxiety plays a role, provided he is tolerant of drugs or susceptible to their pleasures. Even an Irish mind-set about the remarkable qualities of alcohol can play a role, as it most certainly has.

What gets addiction started is one thing; what keeps it going quite another. People take their very first drink for a variety of reasons, but addicts take the thousandth because addiction finds new reasons, supplies new stresses and creates new pressures to justify drug use and continue it. When addiction cannot find a ready-made excuse, it invents one. At some point addiction self-perpetuates, creating whatever motivation it needs to continue, creating the very stuff on which it feeds - not just as the result of growing physical dependence but from the psychological point of view as well. Eventually addiction creates both the chemistry and the psychology it needs to survive.

To become an alcoholic there is one psychological factor which must enter the picture—denial. Quite simply, in order for drinking to continue causing problems, one must deny that it is causing them. The drinker who recognizes that his drinking is a problem will do something about it. Thanks to denial, an addict doesn't recognize the problem and continues drinking. Denial is an essential ingredient. To think that the mere presence of denial proves that an alcoholic is psychologically unstable is a mistake, however. Denial of what is painful and unpleasant is part of the coping repertoire of all human beings. At times denial is a blessing, making it possible for a person to function throughout a traumatic event such as a disaster or the death of a loved one. Denial is, in part, what makes it possible for passengers to board roller coasters and airplanes. Denial helps soldiers face battle. Denial helps mothers face childbirth, especially the second and the third. Denial must have played a part in Columbus' setting sail from Spain in the 1490s, and five hundred years later it must have helped Armstrong, Aldrin and Collins set sail for the moon. Denial helps love become marriage, making it possible for lovers to overlook the flaws in each other, and if it plays no role in first marriages, consider the role it plays in second marriages. Airline passengers, soldiers, mothers, explorers and lovers are not considered in psychological ill health generally. The unfortunate fact is that addicts are lovers. They love their drug. They are not likely to want to find fault with it.

Defense mechanisms are not pathology. They become problematic when they backfire. A woman who knits as a way of dealing with her fear of flying uses a helpful and healthy defense - she gets to her destination with a scarf in the bargain. If she is knitting and trips while getting off the plane, knitting becomes a problem.

An addict's denial may center on nothing more than his drinking and drugging. In other respects he may be a model of how to face reality and deal with it, but when it comes to drinking he is defensive and full of rationalizations. Once started, denial becomes integral to that process in which drinking and problems form a circle.

Alcoholism's Oven

Alcoholism's final ingredients are analogous to those elements involved in bread's rising and baking - a time and a place. That environment plays a role in alcoholism does not mean that there are certain places and certain cities which cause alcoholism, or that certain kinds of jobs cause it. They clearly do not. Family members, companions and friends do not cause alcoholism; neither do cultures, societies, and neighborhoods. Each of these "places," however, can play a role in the process. For instance, a potential alcoholic who grows up in a world in which drinking is part of the regular after-work ritual will find that such a world provides opportunities for everyone to drink on a regular basis, including those susceptible to alcoholism.

Jobs do not cause addiction, but if a job either permits or encourages drinking, then the job plays a role. Family stress does not make a person drink, but it might well provide an excuse to drink and someone to blame it on at the same time. Ovens do not create bread. They provide an ideal place for it to rise and bake.

Take a seed, put it in fertile soil in a sunny location, water it, and it has a chance of becoming a flower. Take a susceptible host, surround him with enablers, give him a drink and a denial system, and there is a chance you might find yourself growing a problem drinker.

A Complex Problem

Alcoholism is not just a set of complex causes; its impact is complex as well. Addicts get sick mentally, emotionally, physically, and even spiritually. Livers swell. Egos swell. Thinking contorts. Feelings distort. Given time, alcoholism takes a susceptible host and turn him into a bitter, cynical, hopeless, mistrustful, unloving, dispirited drunk. No part of the human being is left untouched. Few other problems do as thorough a job.

Complex Effects

The keeper of a small town jail was asked how many of his inmates were in jail because of their alcohol and drug abuse and answered that if he freed the drug and alcohol cases, he could lock the remaining prisoners in the bathroom (his was a more colorful word). If nothing else, addiction makes for trouble.

Alcoholism creates all sorts of problems. It disrupts families and neighborhoods. It is a civic and courtroom problem. It is a headache for legislators and police. It is a national health problem, and it costs business and industry billions of dollars by raising the costs of production and insurance. It scars those children who live with it—scars unhealed well after they have grown up. Addiction is a problem for schools.

Addiction appears on the way to becoming the Pandora's box of the twentieth century.

A Primary Problem: In medicine, "primary" is a word used with two distinct meanings. First, it indicates which of several problems has caused a patient to be hospitalized, and which problem, therefore, is the focus of his treatment. "Primary" is also used to indicate whether a disease has its own cause (is "primary"), or is caused by another disease ("secondary"). The question of whether alcoholism is a disease or a symptom of a disease is essentially a question of whether it is primary or secondary. Those who hold that drinking is symptomatic of a psychiatric disorder believe that it is not primary but secondary. It begs the question, therefore, to assume that alcoholism is primary in order to prove it a disease.

Anyone who has visited a hospital emergency room on Saturday at 2:00 a.m. has seen people who had been functioning the preceding afternoon rendered dysfunctional within hours due to their drinking. From this one might easily conclude that drinking is a primary disorder in the first sense of the word. But is it primary in the second sense? It is the purpose of this entire chapter to demonstrate that chemical dependency is a primary disease, but at this point one thought might teases us into wondering whether alcoholism has its roots in immorality or insanity. Individual psychiatrists and priests have helped alcoholics recover, but in general, psychiatry and religion have had little success dealing with alcoholism. Instead, alcoholics have gotten well from the advice they get from each other. The only group with a track record for recovery is a group of people who have no training in morality or mental health, who would not recognize an "id" from an "ego" if they tripped over them, and who have no expertise in human dynamics and spiritual counseling. But this group has no equal when it comes to abstaining from alcohol and being happy at the same time. Alcoholics Anonymous has the track record for recovery.

That Alcoholics Anonymous has been effective does not establish alcoholism as a disease. What it demonstrates is that treatment administered by professionals is not essential to recovery for everyone. This is not to say that treatment is unimportant. Where denial is adamant, treatment is critical. Where hope is dim, treatment is life saving. And when addiction is complicated by a psychiatric illness, expert treatment is necessary. And one of the ironies of addiction may prove to be that the earlier it is detected, the more we may need people who are specially trained to deal with the denial which accompanies it.

A Drunking Problem

The hypothesis that drinking is a symptom of a psychiatric illness rests on the assumption that the alcoholic's primary problem is psychiatric and his drinking secondary. The thinking goes like this. An addict's problem has to do with his reason or reasons for turning to alcohol. His drinking reveals he has problems while at the same time concealing what that problems might be. Treatment uncovers and resolves an alcoholic's underlying need to drink. Once therapy succeeds and the underlying psychic turmoil is resolved, drinking will no longer be a problem. Drinking, in other words, is not the alcoholic's real problem.

The assumption is half true. An alcoholic does not have a "drinking" problem. His is a "drunking" problem. Exploring why he drinks may intrigue the explorer, but whatever the reason, it is irrelevant to the specific problem he has with alcohol. That problem concerns not his starting; it concerns his persistent failure at its stopping. *Loss of control,* what happens *after* he starts, is at the heart of the alcoholic's problem. For some time Alcoholics Anonymous has captured this core truth in a single sentence: "It's the first drink that gets you drunk."

Some alcoholics understand all too well *the reasons* they drink. They failed in business, or they succeeded at it. They are lonely. They are happy. They are angry. They are depressed. They feel nothing. Family life is boring. The job is stressful. They want out of a loveless marriage. They love to celebrate. They want to escape. They resent their parents. They got promoted. They didn't. They live in an unhappy home. They have been cheated by life. They won. They lost. They didn't get a chance to play. Insight, however, does not solve a drunking problem. Once sober, knowing why he drinks may help an alcoholic avoid the first drink and, thereby, avoid the process. But even with the aid of an understanding psychotherapist, the alcoholic who gains insight into his motivation, the quirks of his personality and the dynamics which shaped his early childhood, is still unable to drink without losing control. In other word, he cannot drink without drunking. What baffles alcoholics is not always their motives; what baffles them is that they end up drunk when they want to and when they don't want to. And so, the question, "why does he drink" misses the point. The pertinent question is "why does he drunk?"

Properly understood alcoholism is A Drunking Problem.

A Chronic Disorder: Alcoholism doesn't go away. It is a chronic disorder. Like other diseases, diabetes for example, alcoholism is not cured; it is arrested. Sober AA members refer to themselves as "recovering" rather than "recovered" to avoid suggesting that their inability to handle alcohol disappears when they are abstinent. Though an abstinent alcoholic will not suffer symptoms while he is abstinent, his condition is chronic; it doesn't go away. He is never cured of his susceptibility. Recovery, therefore, is a process, not an end point.

Not all professionals have accepted alcoholism's chronic nature and have maintained that alcoholics can be retrained as social drinkers (Sobell and Sobell, 1973, 1976, & 1978), that an alcoholic's compulsive drinking is reversible. Others (Pendery, 1982) have refuted that claim. In a re-investigation of twenty alcoholics reported in an earlier study as having mastered the return to controlled drinking (Sobell and Sobell, 1973, 1976, & 1978), researchers found that except for one in a group of twenty, none of the remaining nineteen had been successful at returning to problem-free drinking as had been reported by the earlier study. Eight continued to drink excessively with alcohol-related consequences; six abandoned their attempts at controlled drinking and opted for abstinence as their treatment; one could not be found; and four had died alcohol-related deaths. Not a single dependent subject had become a social drinker (Pendery, 1982).

A Progressive Disorder: Nearly every addiction counselor has seen first hand several cases like the following. A woman was hospitalized for the first time at the end of a twenty-four year drinking history and remained abstinent for twelve years. She resumed drinking, and within one year was hospitalized four times, twice to be detoxified and twice for rehabilitation.

Drinkers who have developed tolerance and who have established a pattern of *loss of control* consistently report that addiction and its symptoms pick up after an abstinent period not where they left off but at a worse stage, suggesting that even during abstinence, addiction's degenerative process progresses unseen. Addiction gets worse in one or all of the following ways:

- The amount and/or frequency of drug use increases;
- The problems caused become more intense and/or more frequent;
- Personality distorts in increasingly troublesome ways.

Though quite often an alcoholic's drinking gets worse; sometimes it is not drinking but the problems it causes which get worse. An individual who was convicted of a single count of driving while intoxicated (DWI) in his first ten drinking years later collects three DWIs in a single year. What used to be "marital discord" becomes "divorce." "Problems at work" turn into "dismissals." The most destructive way in which chemical dependency progresses is in the way it distorts personality. A patient who had been drinking a fifth of whiskey every day for several years was admitted to a hospital and detoxified. In short order his sense of humor returned. He was charming. A year later he relapsed, stayed drunk for six months and was readmitted to the hospital, this time drinking a "mere" pint a day. After this detoxification, however, he was cynical, bitter and resentful. Wrecked lives as well as wrecked livers destroy alcoholics.

If chemical dependency is insidious, complex, chronic, and progressive, which name best accounts for it?

Moral Problem? Those who call chemical dependency a moral problem believe addicts suffer from a sinful disposition, a persistent bad habit, an absence of moral fiber, a lack of values, inadequate upbringing, a weak will, or a defect in character. Excessive drinking, they believe, is a sin or a nuisance at the very least. According to proponents of this hypothesis, an alcoholic has a malicious, misguided, or defective will. His problem is will power, his lack of it. In short, they believe addicts are weak or bad or both.

Only within the past fifty years has alcoholism been considered a disease by other than isolated clusters of people. Even today, generally open-minded people react with disbelief when addiction is called a "disease" because it looks like no other disease they have seen before. Others are not so generous, and some are downright angry. Having been subjected to cruel, abusive, destructive, outrageous, bizarre and criminal behavior they want alcoholics punished not coddled. To them disease seems just another way of letting an alcoholic off the hook. Besides they can explain their anger more easily if they are angry at someone who seems bad rather than someone who is sick. So the notion that addiction is a moral problem is an inviting one.

Exposure Implies Intention?

Proponents of moral problem as an explanation for addiction present several reasons for the hypothesis. They argue that anyone who takes a risk is to blame for whatever results from the risk. The sentiment is expressed in the words, "he brought it on himself" or "he has no one to blame but himself." The implications are interesting. The first is one with which few would disagree, namely, that whoever takes a risk is responsible for dealing with its consequences. If I have an accident while driving my car, I am responsible for repairing the damage - no one else will. The second implication, however, is subtle and illogical. If a disaster results from my taking a risk, it does not mean that I am "to blame" for the disaster. To be responsible and to be to blame are not equivalent and interchangeable. Every time I drive a car, I risk having an accident whether I drive fast or not. If I do have an accident, no one will do what has to be done to have my car repaired except me. But because I am responsible for handling the problem does not mean I intended the problem, that I am "to blame" for it. When I wade into the Atlantic, I risk drowning. Would it follow that if I did drown, that I would be "to blame" for it? Driven to its logical conclusion, reasoning like this holds that those who eat red meat want to have heart attacks, that Damian meant to contract leprosy, and that physicians who treat AIDS patients are subconsciously suicidal.

Solutions Reveal Causes?

Another reason for refusing to accept alcoholism as a disease is based on the presumption that since its cause is unknown, it cannot be called a disease. Proponents argue that since recovery involves neither pills nor surgery nor medical intervention, alcoholism may be called a problem but not rightly labeled a disease. This is a variation on the notion that solutions to problems reveal their causes. In other words, a problem which is solved by an act of will power (the "will" to remain sober) is considered to be caused by the absence of will power, and therefore, not a disease.

The truth is, however, that solutions do not point to their causes all the time. Penicillin cures infection; its absence does not cause it. Some diabetics recover by conforming to a diet; it is an act of will. But because will power solves their diabetes does not mean that lack of will power caused them to be diabetic in the first place. Alcoholics Anonymous' solution is spiritual, but that does not mean alcoholic drinking is sin. What AA has understood is that, having lost a powerful means of altering one's mood, a recovering alcoholic may need an equally powerful replacement.

Only Bad People Do Bad Things?

When people believe that alcoholism is a moral problem, they believe so, in part, because they reason that drunks do bad things. Therefore, they are bad people, and thus alcoholism is a form of badness. There is a simpler explanation. An alcoholic is drugged. A drug-sedated, drug-irritated brain conceives his behavior, and that behavior is then expressed without the benefit of a clear brain's censoring, regulating and inhibiting functions. Such behavior is bound to be distorted. But the dogged persistence that alcohol is truth serum still prompts people to believe that what a person does under its influence reveals the type of person he truly is. The real truth is that alcohol distorts and exaggerates.

Few non-alcoholics want to have their personalities analyzed based on what they said or did in a hospital recovery room after surgery and under sedation. Under such conditions people say and do all sorts of crazy things, uncharacteristic, and atypical of themselves. To analyze someone who is drunk in his living room is to analyze him on similar grounds. To believe that because some alcoholics do bad things, *all* alcoholics have a moral problem, is a leap of several dimensions. Very little can be said of the truth of his moral character when an alcoholic is drunk, except that his behavior is drug-conceived, drug-directed, drug-distorted, and drug-expressed.

Drinking is Voluntary?

There is another, and at first glance, even more compelling reason for presuming alcoholism a moral problem. Drinking appears to be a voluntary act; drug addiction seems self-inflicted. On the surface, it seems as though alcoholics make themselves alcoholics by drinking too much. The conclusion is based on two suppositions. The first is that, since some people do, in fact, control their drinking, all people ought to be able to control it. The second is that since drinking *seems* voluntary, it must *be* voluntary. Those who accept these assumptions interpret excessive drinking as indicating an incorrect, defective, spiteful or malicious will. A few who take this position acknowledge that alcoholism eventually does become a disease, but they believe it was a disease caused by irresponsibility or weakness in the first place.

Drinking Appears Voluntary

No drug has an identical effect on everyone who uses it. Some people find a drug works wonderfully well. Others take it, and it doesn't work at all. And some who take the same drug get sick from it. There is simply no universal single response to drugs. And because alcohol is a drug, human beings are likely to respond to it in a variety of ways. Forces other than will power govern those ways. It is not will which regulates how one responds to a drug. Some people can't handle aspirin; others can't handle Anisette.

If a robbery were videotaped without showing the robber holding the gun, it would appear that a distressed person were giving his money away. When the gun becomes visible, the force which motivates the victim's behavior becomes apparent. Things are not always what they seem. Drinking *seems* voluntary, but the forces which drive it are not always visible.

There is clearly one instance in which the drinking of alcohol does *appear to be* voluntary but is not. Withdrawal develops on a continuum. At some point withdrawal becomes measurable, "visible," whereas, just the week before, the discomfort of withdrawal was present and bothersome but not noticeable to others. In such a condition a drinker appears to choose alcohol, when actually he drinks to calm the jitters of a withdrawal which neither he nor anyone else is able to see. His drinking is an act of self-medication, not of will.

Sub-acute withdrawal explains why someone who is already dependent on alcohol drinks. But why does someone who has yet to reach that stage drink one after another in a relentless, seemingly compulsive way? Why do alcoholics drink too much before they are dependent?

Research with Sons of Alcoholics

Dr. Marc Schuckit's research demonstrates that the sons of alcoholics, even before they are experienced drinkers, perceive, experience and process alcohol differently than the sons of non-alcoholics (see Schuckit and Rayses, 1979; Schuckit et. al., 1981; Schuckit, 1984b). The young men in Schuckit's studies could not have turned themselves into alcoholics because they had not been drinkers long enough to have changed their body's chemistry through drinking. Still they differ from their fellows in three ways:

- They are not as adept at judging the level of their intoxication;
- They build up more acetaldehyde (a potent toxin produced in the breakdown of alcohol), though not enough to cause an aversive Antabuse reaction, and
- They experience a measurably greater degree of the release of muscle tension from drinking than do the sons of non-alcoholics.

In other words, they are not good at knowing how drunk they are. They pay a higher toxic price for drinking. And they get a bigger kick from alcohol than do their peers. Little wonder that ten years down the line they are the ones in a crowd who will say, "one more and I'll go home," and then have six more.

The Alcoholic's Non-Reaction

Another reason certain individuals drink too much is that they can. Nothing helps them stop. Social drinkers have a mechanism which helps them cut off after a couple drinks. Even when they try to keep pace with alcoholics drink for drink, social drinkers get sicker quicker, and they realize this. The wife of an alcoholic made a valiant effort to drink along with her husband in order to keep him company, but found she got sick trying. A husband tried to keep pace with his high tolerance alcoholic wife but found that he was the one carried home. Though they can ignore it, social drinkers have a built-in early warning system about alcohol. One drink makes them feel good, and a second better, but if their blood alcohol level rises further, a social drinker starts to feel, dizzy, groggy, sleepy or sick or unpleasantly out of control. These protective signals warn him that alcohol is a poison, not good for him. If he stops because of these warnings, it is hardly an act of pure self-control. His will does the smart thing; it cooperates with bodily warnings. Social drinkers can choose to drink beyond this point, but they have to have a strong desire to do so. Their chemistry rebels against it.

Unlike social drinkers, alcoholics report no such warnings. To them the first drink feels good; the second better; the third marvelous; the fourth outstanding; the fifth spectacular; and with the sixth they feel on top of the world. They have no rheostat, no bodily rebellion against increasing doses of poison until they have reached levels which would stun elephants. Without a shut off system, an alcoholic never finds it easy to stay within reasonable limits. What is too much booze is guess work. And as long as some booze feels good and more feels better, he will always find it difficult to avoid drinking too much.

Alcoholics have problems not only when they drink too much, they have trouble when they drink too little. In *Under The Influence* Dr. James Milam points out that addiction reaches a point in which it is not his continuing to drink but his stopping which causes an unpleasant feeling and a decrease in performance. At the bar, while imbibing, he is fine. On the way home his blood alcohol falls, and he starts to feel "out of it," and this experience is what impels another drink when he gets home. Though it appears he drinks because he wants to, the truth is he drinks partly to prevent from slipping into the dysfunction caused by too little alcohol in a system accustomed to more (Milam, pp. 52-53).

Anyone who is a poor judge of his intoxication, who has no rheostat to help limit his drinking, and who gets a bigger boost from drinking than others, is likely to have problems controlling how much he drinks.

Future research may provide additional explanations for why some people drink more than others. In the meantime, to assume that excessive alcohol and other drug use is an act regulated solely by the will, uninfluenced by one's bodily response to drugs, begs the question. It is cheating to argue that all drug use is voluntary in order to prove that alcoholism is self-inflicted.

What "Moral Problem" Fails to Explain

Proclaiming addiction a "moral problem" sheds more light on the attitude of the proclaimer than on observations about the illness. It may be comforting to think that good people will not become addicted because they are good, but presuming a "moral problem" fails to explain the wide range of different people, some very good people, who, in fact, do become alcoholic. Any large group of alcoholics is made up of people from so many walks of life with such varied backgrounds, philosophies and upbringings that calling them all weak or bad stretches credibility.

"Moral problem" fails to explain why training of the will, psychotherapy, conversion and moral rehabilitation fail to change an alcoholic's tolerance and impaired control. Calling alcoholism a moral problem fails to explain how someone who is able to pass the most strenuous test a society has ever devised for determining integrity, stamina, determination and will power, who has, in other words, the "right stuff" to be an astronaut, will fail to have the self discipline to control his drinking.

To accept alcoholism as a moral problem requires embracing a whopping set of assumptions. One must believe that from ten to eighteen million people in the United States have developed an identical moral problem. One has to accept that the moral failing these millions have developed will manifest in the same way in all of them, namely, by their inability to handle alcohol. Added to that, one must accept that this particular moral failing will take the same form for athletes and weakling, priests and prostitutes, businessmen and bums, con men and congressmen, free loaders and First Ladies alike. To continue to believe that alcoholism is a moral problem requires that one accept that those alcoholics who have demonstrated remarkable self-control in the other areas of their lives would suddenly exhibit a selective loss of control in a single area.

If alcoholism is a weak person's response to stress, why does it not occur at similar rates among people who have suffered similar stresses? American Indians have had a fair share of stress with high rates of alcoholism, but Jews, who as a group have had as much stress, have a significantly lower rate of alcoholism (Milam, pp. 40-41).

To call alcoholism a disease does not mean that every alcoholic is an innocent. Some alcoholics are anti-social, whether drunk or sober. To call alcoholism a disease does not mean that behavior plays no role in developing an addiction. A drinking problem is impossible without two behaviors, drinking and denying. What calling alcoholism a disease does mean is that the factors which play a role in a developing drinking problem need not be immoral or weak or abnormal or pathological. Even moral and psychologically ordinary people become addicts.

Symptom of an Underlying Disorder? Symptom, a secondary manifestation of an underlying psychiatric disorder, is another name given to alcoholism. Because alcoholism can mimic nearly any psychiatric problem, and because there are alcoholics who exhibit only psychological symptoms (health symptoms and social consequences are minimal or go undetected), it is a small step to conclude that if on the surface a problem *looks* psychological, then underneath it must *be* psychological.

Those who believe the "symptom" hypothesis hold that abusive drinking is caused by unresolved psychic conflict or serious psychiatric illness, that mental-emotional problems are obscured beneath a cloud of alcohol, and that special treatment is needed to resolve them. There are two variations to the hypothesis. One holds that an alcoholic's psychiatric problems cause him to become physically dependent on alcohol, and so he can never drink safely again, even after his psychiatric problems are resolved. The other holds that, once his underlying problems are solved, an alcoholic will drink normally because he will no longer need to abuse alcohol or other drugs. In both versions, however, specialists with years of education about how to access unconscious motivation find interpreting a drinking problem as a problem with drinking too simple.

Some AA members do believe alcoholism is a symptom. They

cite *Alcoholics Anonymous,* their guiding book, as what appears undeniable evidence for it. The "Big Book" says, "Our liquor was but a symptom. So we had to get down to causes and conditions" (p. 64). Out of context the statement seems to say that alcoholism is a manifestation of another problem, that it is secondary. The context, however, does not concern the causes of alcoholism. The context concerns the barriers to overcoming it. "*Getting down to causes"* appears in a discussion of the defects of character which block spiritual recovery as that is defined by a spiritual third step ("Made a decision to turn our will and our lives over to the care of God *as we understood Him*"). At this point the "Big Book" is not citing reasons for an alcoholic's compulsion to drink. Rather, it is elaborating the defects of character, specifically self centeredness, which get in the way of his recovering - which get in the way of his turning his will over to a "Higher Power." An interpretation of this section of *Alcoholics* Anonymous will sound something like this: "Drinking was but one layer of the multiple layers of problems alcoholism created for us. At a deeper level, the resultant self centeredness which our drinking created is what keeps us alcoholics from gaining and maintaining a contact with a Higher Power." There is no reason to believe that the writer of the sentence, "our drinking was but a symptom," was speaking other than metaphorically when he used that word, "symptom." In fact, from the beginning the purpose of the "Big Book" has been to show alcoholics how others recovered, not to provide a treatise on why people become alcoholic in the first place (see the Foreword to the first edition of *Alcoholics Anonymous*).

At first glance, "psychiatric disorder" does appear to account for a drinker's behavior. Alcoholics act crazy when they are drunk. Some act a little "off" on the days between. They can be labile and unpredictable, full of nervous energy one moment and sullen the next. They sulk and brood. In three days they go from depressed to angry to suicidal. They do not look well glued together. And the reason is that they are not well glued together.

"Does an alcoholic look crazy?"
"Yes."
"Why does he look crazy?"

"He *looks* crazy because he *is*."

The next question is the important one.

"Why is he crazy?"

"He is crazy from alcohol. And when he is not crazy *from* it, he is crazy *for* it."

An alcoholic suffers from an illness which involves multiple forces at work on him all at the same time, and these forces can and do make alcoholics look crazy. A drug poisons his brain and distorts his perception. Denial affects his mind. His pursuit of the drug distorts his motivation. His feelings are blunted or exaggerated.

How can an alcoholic's crazy behavior be explained? Ockham's razor is the principle of reasoning which holds that when there are two ways to explain what causes a problem—the one a simple, obvious and straightforward explanation, and the other remote and complicated - that the obvious and immediate explanation be considered true until proven otherwise. Using Ockham's razor, alcoholic drinking by itself can be seen to account for impulsive behavior, irrational behavior, indecisive behavior, persistent anger and resentment, rage, violence, fear, paranoia, anxiety, phobia, mistrust, mood swings, depression, agitation, flat and/or inappropriate affect, memory lapses, outbursts of physical and emotional fury, extreme thinking, vacillation, hypersensitivity, self-centeredness, egocentric thinking, immature responses to rejection, and a sense of entitlement. Less common but still attributable to alcohol and other drugs are hallucinations, delusions and other breaks from reality. As the result of acute intoxication, idiosyncratic intoxication, long term toxicity, and withdrawal, alcoholism is very much what LeClair Bissel, past president of the American Medical Society on Alcoholism, calls it, "the great masquerader" (Drews, p. 134).

An elegantly simple cut of Ockham's razor maintains that since alcohol can cause a drinker's symptoms, it should be thought that it does cause them. The only way to determine whether this is true is to see what happens once alcohol is removed. Many an alcoholic with troubling psychiatric symptoms during active addiction finds those symptoms disappear with abstinent treatment. Some, of course, have psychiatric problems in addition to alcoholism, but those problems can be seen in more accurate dimension after the bloat of alcoholism subsides.

One warning here. Simply to remove alcohol from an alcoholic's life is not to treat his alcoholism. Treatment involves more than just taking the drug away, and yet what it involves is specific to addiction. There is no more lonely, resentful creature in the world than an alcoholic without booze. Total treatment involves dealing with the impact of his years of denial. It involves undoing years of rationalizing. It includes learning how to have fun without drugs. It includes resolving resentments, at the very least - the resentment at being alcoholic and having to treat the problem. Total recovery requires time to overcome guilt and shame. It requires one to reconcile himself to the loss of the drug and the lifestyle which accompanies it. An alcoholic who has done nothing more than stop drinking is an untreated alcoholic. He is dry, not sober.

What "Symptom" Fails to Explain

For anyone who has developed tolerance for alcohol, a discussion of whether addiction has physical or psychological origins is academic. The tolerant drinker cannot drink moderately. Either he drinks to excess to get the kick, or he may as well not drink at all. Some addicts have been tolerant of mood altering drugs from the outset, and calling their problem psychogenic does not explain their early high tolerance. Few alcoholics, very few, in fact, work deliberately at developing tolerance, drinking and drugging until they are good at it. Addicts don't train to become drug tolerant. Some were always tolerant, and others developed it with little effort.

Claiming addiction a problem in which disturbed individuals act out serious psychiatric problems does not explain why, even after years of psychotherapy administered under abstinent conditions by psychiatrists familiar with addiction, a person remains tolerant of alcohol and resumes his use of it with even greater *loss of control* than before psychotherapy. Old-fashioned observation teaches us that addiction is progressive despite psychotherapy, solemn oaths, and even ordination to the priesthood.

Finally, proclaiming alcoholism a psychiatric disorder leaves unexplained how, since the founding of Alcoholics Anonymous, most using AA have resumed healthy and productive lives without the help of psychiatrists.

Still Difficult to Accept: Despite both logic and evidence, it is still difficult to accept alcoholism as a disease. Americans who were raised "to lift themselves up by their bootstraps" (an idiom which, incidentally, had to have been coined by someone who never wore boots) consider alcoholism so easy to solve that it couldn't possibly be a disease, and even if it were a disease, it couldn't be a serious one.

Television viewers laugh at alcoholism, even at advanced cases of it. In one situation comedy popular in the 1980s, the show's funniest character is an itinerant preacher turned taxi driver, who suffers significant brain damage because of alcohol and hallucinogens. It is difficult to laugh at this character, although we do, and at the same time view him as seriously and permanently brain damaged.

When hospitals offer wine as a beverage choice on a patient's lunch menu, it is difficult for the patient and his or her visitors to accept alcohol as a serious drug and alcoholism as a serious disease. Even addicts find it difficult to accept disease as the explanation for addiction - but for different reasons. If an addict considers his problem a disease, he is sure to be terrified by it. Sooner or later, he will find it difficult to delude himself into thinking he can control a disease. Addicts like to think that their problem is in their control, although it is simply that they haven't tried to control it yet. Not really tried, that is.

Non-addicted family members have a hard time with the disease concept too. If they have suffered at the hands of an alcoholic, they are too angry to accept "disease" as explaining the experience. How could someone who is sick have caused them such rage? It is easier to believe that an alcoholic is bad, and that they are angry with him because of that. For the family which does accept alcoholism as a disease, the future is no less frightening. Family members feel even less in control than they did before they accepted alcoholism as a disease.

A Definition of Disease: Definitions of disease are either so broad that any discomfort, even the common cold, qualifies; or so narrow that only one type of illness qualifies. A definition is useful if it avoids extremes. Five elements make up a definition which is specific and flexible. A disease is

- A destructive process
- In an organ or an organism
- With a specific cause or causative factors
- Characteristic symptoms
- Which gets worse if untreated.

If chemical dependency is a disease, it will fit each of these criteria. It does.

A Destructive Process

A disease is a destructive or disruptive process. Chemical dependency is a process. In fact, it is several processes. It is a process of adaptive tolerance and physical dependence (Milam). It is a history of morbidity (Vaillant). It is a progression of interactive, pathological family dynamics (Wegscheider). It is a string of intensifying symptoms (Jellinek).

Chemical dependency is destructive. When characterized by tolerance and loss of control, untreated alcoholism leads in the direction of jail, institutionalization, or death. In Maryland, a state mental hospital named, "Spring Grove," was at one time a domiciliary for chronically impaired, "wet brain" alcoholics. Members of Baltimore AA groups used to describe the active drinker's future as "the Group, the Grove, or the Grave."

Addiction's progression is predictable. Even though symptoms and their sequence vary with individuals, alcoholism progresses from early exposure to symptomatic use to loss of control to problematic use to compulsive drinking and finally to serious morbidity. No one has that crystal ball which foresees recovery's course, but what happens to alcoholics who drink is predictable. It is this predictability, despite the variety of personalities who go through it, which provides persuasive testimony for believing chemical dependency operates as a function of a disease rather than as a function of one's personality.

In an Organ or an Organism

Research from several sources postulates that alcoholics differ from non-alcoholics in bodily and psychological ways, and that these differences are not the consequence of drinking but precede and cause it. When they drink, the sons of alcoholics build up more acetaldehyde than their peers who have no family history of alcoholism (Korsten et. al., 1975). Some research demonstrates that individuals at high risk for alcoholism get more of a kick from drinking and are less able to know when they've had enough than others (Schuckit et. al., 1981 and Schuckit, 1984b). Other research demonstrates that potential alcoholics pay a greater price than their low risk friends, getting sicker livers each time they drink (Lieber, 1976). Milam summarizes animal studies and other research which suggest that acetaldehyde interacts with other brain chemicals to form tetrahydroisoquinolines (THIQ), and that isoquinolines act on opiate receptors in the brain to explain the addictive qualities of alcohol (Milam, 29-42). In one study, tetrahydropapaveroline, produced when dopamine and acetaldehyde combine (remember—alcoholics build up more acetaldehyde than others), was injected into the brains of rats who then chose alcohol over water and drank it until they developed withdrawal-like symptoms (Myers and Melchior, 1977).

Research into the differences between the brain waves of children of alcoholics and peers with no family alcoholism history suggests genetic factors are involved. A brain wave, called P-3, has been known to be deficient in chronic alcoholics, and it was believed that alcoholics destroyed their P-3 capacity by drinking too much. Researchers, however, found differences between the P-3 voltage of boys with a family history and those who had no family history, even though the "high risk boys" were between 7 and 13 years old and had not been given alcohol as part of the experiment (Begleiter et. al., 1984).

In a study of alpha waves, brain waves which are associated with states of well being, sons of alcoholics between 19 and 21 years old, who had themselves not received a diagnosis of alcoholism, produced significantly more alpha waves from drinking than did a similar group of young men with no family history of alcoholism (Pollock et. al., 1983). Those prone to alcoholism may respond differently to alcohol from the outset.

Research continues. Though no single study nails a particular physiological peculiarity as *the* cause of alcoholism, the weight of research suggests that the tendency to become drug tolerant or to use drugs in compulsive or problematic ways is more a matter of one's chemistry than his will. People who can't handle booze seem to have been born prone to that problem.

Alcoholism involves more than can be explained by the way the brain or the liver handles a drug, however. In order for a predilection to compulsive drug use to become full-fledged, in order for cells to adapt to drug, denial must enter the picture. Without denial, no progression! Without progression, no disease! **The simplest definition of an alcoholic is that he is a person with a body that can't handle alcohol and a mind that keeps denying and trying.**

Specific Causative Factors

Clearly we do not have the definitive answer to what causes alcoholism. Research into the other drug dependencies needs to continue as well, though one adoption study of 242 males and 201 females reports three correlates: 1) drug abuse correlates highly with antisocial personality which in turn was predicted from antisocial biologic background; 2) a biologic background of alcohol problems predicts increased drug abuse even in adopted children who do not have antisocial personalities; and 3) environmental factors of divorce and psychiatric disturbance in the adoptive family are associated with drug abuse (Cadoret et. al., 1986). There is research which suggests that personality dimensions, such as "novelty seeking, harm avoidance and reward dependence" may reflect variations in brain systems which modulate behavioral responses to various classes of drugs (Cloninger, 1988, p. 66). What seems a preference for alcohol or cocaine may actually be influenced by underlying genetic mechanisms (Cloninger, 1988).

Until there is a body of research into drug addiction, we may have to go on faith that the other addictions are likely to prove similar to alcohol addiction. Going on faith may not satisfy those who insist that health problems are not legitimately classified as diseases until their causes are known. Such a position, followed to its logical conclusion, however, would prevent medicine from treating certain cancers and schizophrenia. The fact is that physicians do successfully treat diseases for which they have only clues about causes.

Characteristic Symptoms

Alcoholism produces characteristic symptoms, two of which deserve special attention because they are progressive and because a dynamic interaction exists between them: denial and loss of control.

Denial is that mechanism by which the mind defends itself against a reality too painful to tolerate. *Loss of control* describes the phenomenon in which a first drink, snort, or dose sets off a string of doses which leads to unintended intoxication and unpredictable behavior. Denial and *loss of control* work in tandem. An alcoholic loses control and then denies it. Instead of seeing impaired control as the reason for his getting sick or drunk, he blame it on stress, family problems, the price of a good time, bad clams, shrimp, crabs or lobster (shell fish take more than their fair share of the blame for vomiting), too much or too little to eat, mixing drinks, a disappointment in business, rejected love, or a death in the family. Instead of being alarmed by his lack of control, he explains it away.

When *loss of control* is coupled with its denial, alcoholism is set on a progressive course. From that point on an addicted person is not likely to see that he has a problem until it causes so much pain and trouble that even he can't avoid considering his inability to control alcohol the reason for his "drunking." For the process to end, forces outside the drinker must intervene. Addictive drinking and drugging is compulsive, plain and simple. Some never accept that. Some never see it.

Summary: If "disease" is defined as a condition in which a bodily susceptibility ("X" factor), coupled with behavior (drinking and denial of problems related to it), leads to morbidity (sickness and problems), despite an individual's will (demonstrated by repeated failure at controlled use), then "disease" is the best name we have for what happens to alcoholics.

5

SELF DECEPTION AND SELF DIAGNOSIS

"Diagnosis" comes from ancient Greek, and the word means to know something "clean through." Diagnosing is a doctor's task, and given the complexity of the health care field, only a trained professional can make a diagnosis in many cases. Chemical dependency, however, is different. It is a disease for which the patient makes the critical diagnosis, not the doctor. It is peculiar in another sense too. Treatment for alcoholism begins not after its diagnosis is made as with other diseases. Treatment begins the moment the patient asks himself this question, "Am I an alcoholic?"

Self Diagnosis: Recovery from chemical dependency is based on this axiom: **No one solves a problem he does not have.** The first step to solving a problem is to *have* one. Applied to health care, the axiom means that patients comply with the recommended treatment only if they believe they have the disease for which the treatment is recommended. Applied to alcoholism, this means that recovery begins when a drinker makes his first honest attempt to determine if drinking causes his problems.

Self-diagnosis is a long and difficult road. First, an alcoholic must stop blaming others and acknowledge that it is his behavior which is a problem. Only after he accepts this is he ready to consider whether drinking plays a part in the problem - at the very least that his drinking is tangent to that problem. Next, he must conclude that drinking causes problems. And finally he must realize that drinking causes problems not by chance but because he is not in control of his drinking. He is "powerless." A doctor may tell a patient that he *appears* powerless, but only the patient knows it *"clean through."*

Self-diagnosis is so important that Alcoholics Anonymous twelve step program begins with it:

> **"We admitted we were powerless over alcohol: that our lives had become unmanageable."**

Recovery begins when an alcoholic acknowledges that his life is "unmanageable," and that will power by itself fails to solve his problem.

"At Gut Level": Addiction goes "clean through." Its denial goes deep. Self-diagnosis is not a casual musing. It is a gut level conviction. The following statements might seem honest self assessment, but a closer look reveals they have little to do with diagnosis, nothing to do with disease, and even less to do with addiction.

I drink too much.
I have a drinking problem.
I have a mild case of alcoholism.
My family thinks I have a problem.
I get drunk too often.
When I drink, I have problems.
I should stop drinking or drug taking.
I am ashamed of my drinking.
I feel guilty about it.

None of these statements says "I am powerless, " and when a life of abstinence is the next step, only gut level awareness of powerlessness will provide the basis for that step. The individual who succeeds at it sounds very different:

I have tried will power. Will power doesn't work. My drinking is beyond that.

I don't *have* alcoholism; I *am* alcoholic.

This is not a habit; it's a compulsion.

My addiction is not in a bottle. It is in me.

No one is to blame. No one made me this way. I didn't try to become alcoholic, but that is what I am.

My problem doesn't come and go; it keeps getting worse.

The conviction that I am powerless is based on my track record with alcohol and drugs.

I am powerless. After a first drink (dose, hit, snort), my drinking is unpredictable. Will power by itself cannot keep me from that first one.

In AA the slogan, "the soberer you get, the drunker you were" suggests that recovery is a process, that denial erodes, and that acceptance is a dawning. In fact, acceptance sometimes takes years and continues well into abstinent recovery. Professionals who work with addicts in the early stages of treatment frustrate themselves when they try to force that process. At the beginning a professional helps the patient see the need to take a hard look at his drinking. He can point out the wisdom of remaining abstinent while doing so. He can help the patient sort through layers of denial. But self-diagnosis is so scary a process that it cannot be rushed.

There has been interest in the treatment community in the topic of relapse. Books are written about it. Treatment centers offer programs designed specifically for relapsed patients. Workshops teach counselors how to identify it and intervene in it. Theories about it are plentiful. Not enough is said, however, about the one feature which plays a major role in relapse during early recovery: failure at gut level self-diagnosis. There may be plenty of reasons an alcoholic may *want* to drink, but the chief reason he *does* drink is that he believes he can get away with it. In his mind there is little risk involved in fooling with alcohol. He supposes he will manage intoxication and stop when he must.

Any alcoholic who claims he will have a little slip and get back to recovery believes he is in control of the slip. He does not consider himself powerless. And that's denial, plain and simple.

Any therapist who works in a psychiatric hospital is familiar with the addicted patient hospitalized for treatment of a mental or emotional disorder a year or more after he has gotten sober. A number of these dually afflicted patients know well that no matter how painful their psychiatric problems, they cannot afford to drink to relieve them. Though they need relief, hospitalization is more acceptable than drinking as a way to get relief. These patients know at gut level they cannot control drinking. Their recovery is based on the conviction that they are powerless. They also convince the rest of us that powerlessness over alcohol is not synonymous with helplessness.

Keeping It Simple: The question of whether one is an addict is difficult enough without cluttering the mind with other questions which confuse the issue and subvert the candor of the process. Self-assessment is more likely to be an honest process if its focus is as simple as this,

Am I an alcoholic?

Two other questions, if considered simultaneously, cloud the issue. "What is alcoholism; is it a disease?" And, "Will I do anything about it; will I stop drinking and seek help?" If one asks himself these questions at the same time he is trying to figure out whether he is alcoholic, his answers to questions about symptoms will be complicated at least, and probably distorted. The reason is simple. If someone suspects his problem is a moral problem, he is likely to be too ashamed to admit it. If he decides ahead of time that either he cannot or will not stop drinking, he will virtually be forced into deceiving himself about whether he is symptomatic for a disease which requires abstinence. Few people want to regard themselves as intentionally self-destructive, which indeed they would be if they refused to treat a fatal disease. It is easier on the psyche to believe that one does not have a disease than to believe one does but refuse to do anything about it. Finally, those who believe alcoholism is a psychiatric disorder may be convinced that they drink to relieve its pain. For self-assessment to be an honest process, it has to be a simple one.

Requirements For Self-Assessment: Chemical dependency requires three conditions in the person trying to self diagnose: honesty, willingness, and abstinence. Since denial plays so key a role in addiction, self-diagnosis requires one to double his efforts at self honesty. Blackouts, repression and euphoric recall make an alcoholic's memory not the most useful tool in reconstructing his past, and so he may need help from others to reconstruct it accurately.

Willingness! The question of whether one is an alcoholic cannot be answered as a favor to someone else—because a family member or a judge thinks it wise. An alcoholic must answer the question for himself and for no reason other than that knowing the truth is critical.

Dry! Clean and sober is the only condition for a brain to be in while its owner tries to decide if he is addicted. The diagnostic decision is literally a *vital* one, and life and death issues are best considered undrugged. Alcoholism counselors generally recommend a drug free period of ninety days while the individual is self-assessing. And if someone tries to remain abstinent for ninety days but fails, he has a problem. His problem is that he has not done what he has wanted to do, and at the very least will have to wonder why. Addiction may be the answer.

Another reason it is important to abstain while self-diagnosing is not so obvious. There is an inherent contradiction in the person who believes that he decides to drink while he is trying to figure out if his drinking is, in fact, compulsive. The person who "decides" to drink has already concluded that his drinking is volitional, an act of will. He already believes that drinking is a choice he makes. In that frame of mind he cannot conclude that drinking is also compulsive. It simply cannot be both a *decision* and a *compulsion* at the same time.

The Difficulties of Self Diagnosis: Addiction is tough to recover from because self-diagnosis is not only a requisite process; it is a devilishly difficult one. Six features make it so:

- The very brain which the drug has affected is the brain which must be used to determine whether an individual has a drug problem.
- To become an addict, one must cultivate a denial system, and so a mind which has learned to deny the problem must be used to assess the problem.
- Addiction is insidious; it is hard to diagnose even by experts.
- Community drinking customs make distinguishing normal from abnormal drinking difficult.
- A defensive mind becomes proficient at maneuvering, and this keeps addicts in denial.
- Fear and pride make self-diagnosis traumatic.

An Affected Brain

Chemical Dependency is perverse. The addict in search of his symptoms is a person reviewing drugged experience with a drug-affected brain. The very memory which the disease distorts is the memory which must be used to reconstruct its history and diagnose it. Memories filter through the haze of a drug. Blackouts interfere with the process, and it is impossible to interpret the meaning of an experience if one has no memory of having had the experience in the first place. Many experiences which an alcoholic does remember happened while he was drunk, and so his version of them is different from the version of others who were sober at the time. The same incident recalled by two heads, one clear and the other fogged, is recalled quite differently. Similarly, alcoholics are often surprised to learn that others viewed their drunkenness as extreme when they thought they had hidden it quite well. Recovering alcoholics find photographs taken of them when they were drunk and are amazed at how "out of it" they looked, although at the time they thought they were quite debonair.

An Affected Mind

What makes self-diagnosis doubly perverse is that addiction cannot develop unless one learns to deny it. Self-deception becomes an established mechanism in the very mind which must get past self-deception. An alcoholic believes it when he says,

> I am not an alcoholic.
>
> I do not even have a very big problem.
>
> I may have a problem, but it will pass. It's a phase.
>
> If it does not pass, it has nothing to do with drinking. I need counseling, but not for drinking.
>
> If it does concern drinking, I'm not addicted to alcohol. I just drink too much.
>
> Even if it is alcoholism, I can handle it. I don't need help.

The major difference between smart alcoholics and dumb ones is that smart ones stay sicker longer. Those good at semantic maneuvering and subtle distinctions have abundant means for prolonging denial. Intelligence is no advantage in getting through denial. It has proven a fatal disadvantage.

A Subtle and Insidious Process

Diagnosing alcoholism is difficult also because by its nature it is insidious - difficult to see. Alcoholism progresses in one of two ways: either so gradually that it is imperceptible, like aging, or so quickly (for some symptoms have been present from the outset of drinking) that it seems normal, common, not extraordinary at all. Instant alcoholics, so-called because they have been symptomatic from their earliest use, fail to consider themselves as having a drinking problem because their drinking has always been the same. It takes a while to realize one's behavior is abnormal when one has never known normal.

Community Customs

Community custom plays a role in making self-assessment difficult. Extreme versions of alcoholism have always been better box office draw at the movies than the stories of garden-variety alcoholics. A functioning alcoholic will fail to diagnose himself if he fails to fit what society presents on screen as a template for alcoholism. When television depicts heavy drinking as an accepted part of American socializing, that muddles the distinction between social drinking, heavy drinking and pathological drinking. In addition, every so often television situation comedies present pathological drinking as commonplace and funny. Finally, alcoholics drift toward each other. In a room of abnormal drinkers, abnormal drinking seems normal. In short, a community helps addicts deny the problem by a patchwork of community denial, including the very way society perceives and presents normal alcohol use.

The Habit of Defensiveness

A disease which involves an increasingly intensive system of denial creates reasoning which is convoluted, and an approach to semantics and causation which splits hairs. Addicts get quite concrete and literal when it comes to questions about their drinking. They miss the intent of a question by focusing on a single word, so fixed on the nuance of a word that they miss the intent of a sentence.

Alcoholics Anonymous distributes twenty questions to those trying to self-diagnose. According to the accompanying instructions, if one question is answered "yes," it is a warning that you are alcoholic. Two "yes" answers, and chances are that you are alcoholic. Three or more questions answered affirmatively and you are "definitely" alcoholic. In the thick of denial an addict answering those twenty questions sounds like a defense attorney. For instance, when asked whether he loses time from work *due to drinking,* he answers that he loses time *due to sickness* but not due to drinking, somehow convincing himself that a "yes" answer would mean that he missed work because he had gotten drunk that morning.

Question 7 asks, "Do you turn to lower companions and an inferior environment when drinking?" The evasive answer is that he doesn't "*turn*" to such companions; he just "e*nds up*" there. He might even counterattack by claiming that anyone who calls his companions lower is a bigot.

Question 10 asks if he craves a drink at a definite time daily, and is answered "no" by an alcoholic whose image of craving is so extreme—eyes bugged out, tongue drooping, crawling on hands and knees, and drooling—that no one would fit such a description. Craving is pictured in whatever way does not fit the answerer.

Question 16—"Do you drink alone"? The question is answered "no" if anyone at all is home, even though they are asleep. It is possible to drink alone at the Rose Bowl in the midst of 80,000 people. Lone drinking happens frequently in bars, in fact.

The twenty questions are reprinted here. Take the test.

1. Do you lose time from work due to drinking?
2. Is drinking making your home life unhappy?
3. Do you drink because you are shy with other people?
4. Is drinking affecting your reputation?
5. Have you ever felt remorse after drinking?
6. Have you gotten into financial difficulties as a result of drinking?
7. Do you turn to lower companions and an inferior environment when drinking?
8. Does your drinking make you careless of your family's welfare?
9. Has your ambition decreased since drinking?
10. Do you crave a drink at a definite time daily?
11. Do you want a drink the next morning?
12. Does drinking cause you to have difficulties in sleeping?
13. Has your efficiency decreased since drinking?
14. Is drinking jeopardizing your job or business?
15. Do you drink to escape from worries or troubles?
16. Do you drink alone?
17. Have you ever had a complete loss of memory as a result of drinking?
18. Has your physician ever treated you for drinking?
19. Do you drink to build up your self confidence?
20. Have you ever been to a hospital or institution on account of drinking?

Clarification of a few questions might be helpful. Question 2 may be answered differently by a drinker than by his spouse and children. Consider how family members would answer that and some of the other questions. When Question 5 asks if you have ever felt remorse after drinking, one should answer "yes" if he felt guilty not only about *how much he drinks* but also about his behavior when under the influence.

To answer Question 6, one must consider not only how much money he spends for alcohol but also how much he spends on the lifestyle which goes with it, along with the cost of repairing the damage done by drinking, and the cost of necessary health care due to it. Addicts are shocked when they add up the hidden costs of a single year of addiction.

For Questions 9 and 13 it is necessary to take a long look back at an entire history to see what has happened to ambition and efficiency over that time.

Concerning Question 10, if one has difficulty seeing he craves a drink at a definite time, he should consider how he acts and feels if deprived of it at that time.

Question 11 doesn't ask if you have a drink; it asks if you want one. Many an alcoholic considers himself a problem drinker but not an alcoholic if he has gotten by without an eye-opener though he both needed and wanted it.

Question 12 is easy to gloss over. The question tries to get at whether drinking interferes with normal sleep in any way. Additional questions along the same lines include the following: Do you have trouble falling asleep unless you take a drink or a drug? Do you awaken in the middle of the night feeling nervous, needing something to calm you down so you can get back to sleep? Do you fall asleep and awaken, or do you pass out and come to?

"Yes" is the answer to Question 14 for anyone who has lost his job because of drinking. "Yes" also applies to anyone whose job performance or business judgment has been affected by drinking. "Yes" is the appropriate answer for anyone who is more preoccupied with drinking than with his job.

Anyone who has been admitted to a hospital for the treatment of alcoholism should answer Question 20 in the affirmative, as it should be by anyone who has been treated in an emergency room because of a drunken accident at home, at work, or in a car.

There is nothing fool proof about a pencil and paper test. Tests do not make decisions; test takers do. One's score on this test is simply the sum of the number of times he or she has said "yes" to significant symptoms of alcoholism. The important conclusion is the one the test taker reaches after he knows his score.

There are, of course, people who are so suggestible that no matter what test they take, they end up believing they have the pathology the test is supposed to reveal. Suggestible people should get help from an addiction's specialist rather than trust their own judgment in the assessment process. But because denial is so strong in chemical dependency, there is a greater chance that a self-report questionnaire will fail to diagnose thousands who have the disease than over-diagnose thousands who don't.

Fear and Pride

Finally self-diagnosis is fraught with fear and pride, powerful feelings which make the process stressful. Given alcoholism's reputation, few people eagerly admit to having it. Centuries ago, Sophocles called pride the great destroyer of men. Today it destroys its share of alcoholics. Fear also plays a role. The future for a recovering alcoholic is a life of abstinence, and some alcoholics avoid starting the diagnostic process because they are afraid they are incapable of doing what that process requires.

Proof Positive? Alcoholics are visible. Alcoholism is not. The naked eye can see addictive behavior, but what the eye sees is not addiction itself. One can be certain he has a scarred liver, but cirrhosis is the result of alcoholism, not alcoholism itself. There is yet no way to observe this disease directly. There is no organ which when examined under a microscope either proves or disproves the presence of alcoholism. Some souls are tortured by the debate about whether they are alcoholic. They yearn for direct, positive, unequivocal, physical evidence to decide the issue for them once and for all. No such evidence exists. It may never. The only certainty one can have is moral certainty.

Some of alcoholism's symptoms are telling and almost always point to that diagnosis. Delirium Tremens (DTs), a profound complication of withdrawal, does not happen on a regular basis to non-alcoholics. DTs virtually clinch the diagnosis, but DTs occur in a small percentage of cases, and even among that number, incredible as it seems, there are some who have suffered DTs who still resist believing they are alcoholic. They reason that other medical problems might cause them to be delirious, shaky, dehydrated, hallucinatory and disoriented. Such reasoning would astonish emergency room doctors if it were rare.

Alcoholism is like the sun, too bright to look at. Nevertheless one can be certain the sun is in the sky even though one cannot look at it directly. He knows it through the shadows it makes, through the heat it generates, and through its reflection in windows. The only certainty we can have of alcoholism's presence is the same—through signs.

Two Common Mistakes: An alcoholic looks for loopholes. Anyone who plows through the symptoms presented in the next chapter should be warned about two mistakes alcoholics commonly make. The first is to confuse symptoms with causes. The erroneous thinking goes something like this:

> Alcoholics wreck cars.
> I have never wrecked a car.
> Therefore, I am not an alcoholic.

The fallacy of the logic is that it assumes that all alcoholics wreck cars, and that it is the wrecking of a car which makes one an alcoholic. Alcoholics do not become alcoholics because they smash cars; they wreck cars because they are alcoholic. Drinking in the morning does not cause alcoholism. It works the other way around.

The second mistake is an all or nothing approach, that is, if one doesn't have *all* of the symptoms of a disease, then he doesn't have the disease. A drinker who fits every criterion in the Diagnostic Manual for substance dependence except one is very likely to focus on that one, he concludes he is diagnosis free. In a list of seventy-five symptoms a denying alcoholic is drawn to the one symptom which he has not experienced and looks to it as the *absolute*, the *sine-qua-non* of alcoholism. Alcoholics who do not drink in the morning consider morning drinking the "real" symptom of alcoholism.

No single symptom clinches the diagnosis. The absence of a single symptom does not rule alcoholism out, nor does the presence of a single symptom automatically rule it in. A pattern of symptoms provides the basis for the diagnosis.

Only on the basis of a broad pattern of symptoms and good history taking is a trained diagnostician able to avoid mistaking alcoholism for depression or vice-versa. Poor appetite, sleep difficulty, suicidal ideation, loss of pleasure, slowed response, impotence and depressed mood might indicate that an individual suffers either from an affective disorder, such as depression, or from a substance abuse disorder, such as alcoholism. By themselves these symptoms are not conclusive. Only when they are accompanied by other symptoms, such as tolerance, blackouts, liver disease, legal difficulties and marital problems caused by drinking, is it reasonable to conclude that alcoholism plays the causative role. And for an alcoholic who becomes depressed after a period of treated abstinence, it is critical to his well-being and his sobriety to treat his depression as existing in addition to his alcoholism rather than instead of it.

Alcoholism is capable of imitating every one of depression's usual symptoms. What appears to be depression is sometimes so indistinguishably intertwined with and clouded by alcohol and drug use that only a period of total abstinence under the supervision of a psychiatrist *familiar with the ordinary depression that occurs in early recovery* will clarify whether a patient suffers from depression, alcoholism, or both.

Alcoholism's diagnosis can be tricky.

6

SIGNS AND SYMPTOMS

Blackouts and seizures are symptoms of alcoholism. So are guilt and pancreatitis. Addiction causes trouble at home and at work. It keeps police departments busy. It affects health.

Categories of Symptoms: Alcoholism produces such a range of symptoms that their sheer number and variety easily overwhelm anyone trying to wade through them in order to figure out whether he or she is alcoholic / drug addicted. Some symptoms occur because drugs affects the human brain, others because addiction creates behaviors typical of it. There are symptoms that suggest that drinking interferes with one's ability to perform his expected social roles and responsibilities. Drugs create health problems. The following categories are intended to simplify symptoms according to five types:

Nervous system symptoms are those which arise because mood-altering drugs affect the brains of susceptible individuals in unusual and pathological ways. Tolerance and withdrawal are symptoms of this type.

Behavioral is a name given to symptoms which indicate that someone thinks, feels, and acts like someone who has alcoholism.

Conflict signs—When a person is conflicted about his drinking, that conflict signifies a problem.

Social Consequences—As addiction progresses, it interferes with one's ability to perform his role as citizen, family member, employee and student.

Health Consequences—Abusive drug use damages the body.

Some symptoms fit easily into the above categories; others do not, and a few symptoms can be placed in more than one category. Depression and paranoia, for example, result either from the effect drugs have on the brain or from the impact addiction has on the mind over a period of years. Psychiatrists rightly conclude that drugs cause paranoia and depression if those problems disappear when drugs are stopped. And if the problems persist after abstinence, the affected individual either has additional problems along psychological lines, or his depression and paranoia are the lasting scars of years of drug addiction.

Suicidal behavior might be listed as a "nervous system" sign since some addicts report feeling suicidal only while under the influence of a drug. However, when someone has lost his job, his family, and his self respect because of drinking, he may be suicidally depressed many weeks after he has gotten sober. Relief drinking and outbursts of anger fit several categories as well.

Nervous System Symptoms: Drugs affect the nervous system in ways which indicate that one's use of them is abnormal. When someone flies into a rage from drinking a sedative drug, such as alcohol, that ought to clue the drinker that his response to a depressant is not normal. The development of drug tolerance means an individual is adapting to a drug in a way which is bound to cause problems in the future, if it hasn't done so already. Symptoms of withdrawal are proof positive that an individual has become so dependent that he must maintain a drug level or suffer discomfort. Overdose is an extraordinary experience. When it happens repeatedly, it must be considered symptomatic of a larger problem.

Different classes of drugs produce similar symptoms but in different ways. Alcohol, for instance, causes hallucinations when someone dependent on it stops drinking abruptly. Stimulant drugs users hallucinate because they ingest too much of a drug, not because they stopped it. Physically dependent alcoholics get shaky when their level of alcohol drops, but cocaine snorters gets shaky because they snort too much.

Nervous system signs include:

Increased Need—Over time an addict needs more of a drug than he did previously, and so he or she drinks before a party, gulps or sneaks a drink. He hides his drinking, embarrassed by how much he drinks. He avoids non-drinking situations and seeks drinking ones. He craves, needs, or uses alcohol daily.

Loss of Control describes that phenomenon in which an initial drink, snort or dose starts a process which ends in acute and unintended intoxication and unpredictable behavior. *Loss of control* is more apparent with some drugs than with others, more apparent, for instance, with cocaine than with marijuana. In a single night a cocaine addict may snort what was meant to last a weekend. *Loss of control* is progressive; it worsens over time. It is the reason alcoholics wind up drunk at the wrong time in the wrong place. It explains why they drink more than they promise, and why they are unable to predict on any occasion how much they will drink, for how long, or with what result.

Tolerance—One is tolerant of alcohol if he needs more of it to produce a desired effect, or when the same dose produces less effect than it did previously. Even alcoholics who report a high tolerance at the outset of drinking nevertheless report increased tolerance over the years. It is impossible to determine if someone is drug tolerant on the basis of the effect a drug has from one night to the next since several factors influence how drunk one *feels* on any given occasion. Tolerance is presumed only when, with the same drug potency, rate of consumption, physical health, mind set, setting, and period of years, it takes more drug to get high. Eventually tolerance reverses, and low doses produce dramatic results. Someone who claims booze has stopped working is actually acknowledging that he has become tolerant.

Blackouts—Blacking out is not passing out. A blackout is a period of amnesia while under the influence. In a blackout a drinker does not remember several hours of an evening or driving home or both. Blackouts may be dramatic or uneventful, two hours of an evening or a trip of several days and hundreds of miles missing from memory. Blacked out experiences are never recalled.

Relief Drinking—To use alcohol or another "recreational" drug for its tranquilizing effect is called relief drinking because it is using a "social" drug as if it were a "prescription" drug. Whatever else it might be called, relief drinking is not social drinking. To drink in order to calm down, to induce sleep or to relieve depression is to use alcohol as sleeping pill, tranquilizer, or antidepressant. Someone who regularly drinks before a public performance or lovemaking ought to wonder if such drinking points to a problem. The irony of relief drinking is that much of it aims at relieving problems which drinking has created over time.

Jekyll-Hyde Reaction—Jekyll-Hyde describes a sudden change in personality while consuming alcohol. It is not to be confused with "personality change," which is discussed later. Jekyll-Hyde describes the sudden onset of rage, especially alarming from someone for whom it is atypical when sober. Outbursts of anger and brush fire fury are peculiar responses to a sedative drug.

Impotence and Decreased Interest in Sex—The notion that alcoholic women are nymphomaniacs is a male fantasy. Both men and women may be less inhibited love makers because of booze, but from a biomechanical point of view they are not better performers because of it. They think they are better sex partners when "looped" for the same reason that they think they are better drivers. The truth is they are simply less uptight, not better performers. In advanced stages, alcoholics have another love.

Suicidal Behavior—In early addiction suicidal behavior is usual only when an individual is drunk. Later on, suicidal thoughts, gestures and attempts happen even when one is abstinent because of the mounting effects of drug and shame and loss.

Cognitive Problems—Short-term memory deficits, all or nothing thinking, indecision, and shortened attention signify chemical dependency's damaging effect on the brain.

Emotional Augmentation—Emotional augmentation describes overreaction to stress or sadness - overly intense feelings in situations not connected in a personal way to the individual. Feelings are intensified by a drug-agitated nervous system.

The Shakes—Individuals who are withdrawing from a sedative drug get the shakes, experienced initially as inner tremulousness, but eventually visible as hand tremors. When caused by alcohol, shakes begin twenty-four hours after the last drink. With other depressants, withdrawal's onset may be delayed for as long as seven to nine days. Stimulant drug users feel shaky from too much stimulant.

Convulsions—Seizures may occur during sedative drug withdrawal. They look and sound like epileptic "fits." Seizures also occur from excessive doses of stimulants.

Hallucinations—During sedative withdrawal, an individual may "see" and "hear" things which are not there. Hallucinations result from excessive doses of stimulants as well.

Delirium Tremens: ("DTs") - DTs are more than an hallucinatory experience combined with shakes. Delirium Tremens describes a profound medical condition, confusion, disorientation, a medical crisis, a life threatening complication of alcohol withdrawal.

Fear—A sense of "impending doom," the feeling one is losing his mind, an overwhelming sense of panic, gripping fear that a catastrophe is imminent—all indicate a drinker or drugger is suffering from the long-term effects of drugs.

The Behavioral Signs: Symptoms are called behavioral because they represent how alcoholics and addicts behave during addiction. They are the psychological results of chemical dependency.

It is a mistake to think that because chemical dependency produces psychological symptoms, underlying psychological problems cause it. A diabetic in crisis looks psychologically disturbed, but he is not. Addicts behave strangely under the influence of drugs. Depression and paranoia do result from the toxic effect drugs have on a human brain as much as from the inner turmoil which addiction produces. More often than not, the causes of an addict's behavior are twofold: biochemical and emotional. When someone's emotional well being depends on his using drugs, he will act in all sorts of unusual ways just to get drugs. If, in addition, he needs drugs to stave off withdrawal, his behavior may be downright bizarre.

Psychological or behavioral signs include:

Denial—Denial is not the product of stupidity. Denial is the mechanism the mind uses to keep painful truth at bay. Alcoholics minimize their drinking and trivialize the problems and feelings resulting from it. Their memories of unpleasant experiences and past confrontations are suppressed, even repressed. Denial means that an addict fails to perceive that he has a problem; it does not mean that he knows the truth and deliberately lies.

Rationalization—When compulsion is its cause, a drinker must create all sorts of excuses for why he drinks and drugs as much and as often as he does. Alcoholics blame drinking and drunkenness on all sorts of people, places and things. Quite understandably addicts believe their problems cause their drinking and drug use rather than the other way around.

Projection—When a person finds in himself a trait he despises, he is likely to reject that trait psychologically. The mind, however, will not always allow him to get away with it, and so he ends up seeing that trait in others. This is projection. An angry alcoholic sees other drunks as angry. He sees drinking itself as an expression of anger. Some alcoholics are adept at diagnosing alcoholism in others.

Sensitivity about One's Use - Drinking eventually becomes a touchy subject, and alcoholics will stop bragging about their drinking and start lying about it.

Anxiety—Attacks of worry, fear that they will be "found out," free-floating anxiety characterize alcoholics and addicts.

Ego-Centeredness—After years of swinging between the grandiosity and the humiliation which out of control drinking creates, addicts become ego centered. A "great big I" and a "poor little me" are ego extremes. Sober periods are excruciatingly self-conscious for some.

Depression—Depression is one of the masks alcoholism wears. Even for a garden variety alcoholic, depression may come about because of drug use, because of the cumulative losses he has suffered and/or because of the impact addiction has on confidence and self-esteem. Alcoholism imitates all of depression's clinical symptoms: loss of appetite due to stomach irritation, disturbed sleep due to withdrawal, impotence, suicidal thinking, and loss of interest and energy.

Low Self Esteem—Alcoholics eventually feel worthless, inadequate, and even self-hating. Low self-esteem sometimes hides behind bravado and superficial confidence.

For some addicts, work achievement and career success compensate for feelings of worthlessness. For others, the impact addiction has on self-esteem is obvious.

Loss of Confidence - This problem becomes obvious when one believes he can no longer do what he used to do with ease.

Personality Changes - Not the Jekyll-Hyde reaction mentioned earlier, but a more gradual change in personality which occurs over years. Addicts become moody, apathetic, sarcastic, self-pitying, resentful, depressed, grandiose, antisocial, bitter and cynical.

"Telephonitis" - Intoxicated, often late at night, addicts call up their friends and relatives. The reasons appear to be three-fold: as an attempt to break free from the isolation one feels ("I had to talk to someone"); as a cry for help, and as a means of dissipating feelings of guilt. Sometimes the call is made in a blackout.

Control Ploys - As control erodes, alcoholics try a range of ploys to limit drinking and avoid acute intoxication. A common ploy is to postpone drinking until after 6:00 p.m. or to limit it to weekends. A list of such ploys is included in Chapter 7.

Maturation Problems - Addiction arrests emotional growth. Incredible as it seems, there are addicts who have never interacted at a social gathering without a drink or drug for their entire adult lives. Some have never experienced an emotion from beginning to end without being under the influence somewhere along the line. When feelings are learned under the influence, even alcoholics who are competent in the business world wind up feeling emotionally immature, emotionally younger than their business acumen and their chronological years would indicate. As addiction progresses, maturity regresses, and addicts become demanding, stubborn and immature - the terrible twos in the terrible forties.

Resentment - Resentment is anger's first cousin. It is re-feeling old anger from a past injustice or injury. Resentment may be genuine and justified or exaggerated, even imagined; but whichever it is, resentment plays an interesting dual role in chemical dependency which is discussed in Chapter 7.

Self-Pity - Self-pity is the "poor me" feeling. It looks at what is missing from our lives. Self-pity is often a mask which resentment wears; beneath self-pity lies resentful feelings toward the people and institutions believed responsible for injustice and injury.

Suspiciousness - Suspiciousness in alcoholics can reach paranoid levels. Some carry guns because of it.

Mistrust - Those who hide their feelings are liable to believe that others do the same, thus suspecting the sincerity of others. Hypocrisy which is despised in oneself is projected onto others, further complicating trust. Their own increasing cynicism leads alcoholics to question the motives of others.

Obsession with Alcohol/Drugs - This is another symptom which gets progressively worse over time. It starts out as preoccupation and ends up as obsession. Drinking, once merely one of life's recreations, becomes its main activity.

Inner Conflict: The clash between drunken behavior and personal values gives rise to another set of signs. Social drinkers are not ashamed of how much or how often they drink. Addicts are, and it is this shame which indicates that their drinking is abnormal. The following are signs of addiction because they reveal that guilt and shame. Attempts to deal with those feelings characterize one's drinking.

Guilt—Guilt about drinking, its amount and frequency, as well as outrageous, immoral, and/or illegal behavior point to an alcohol or other drug problem.

Shame—is the emotion one experiences when he believes he has transgressed his own principles and is afraid others will find out. Shame results not only from what alcoholics do when they are drunk but also from what they fail to do because of their preoccupation with drinking.

Remorse—From Latin, "remorse" means "to die again." It is the persistence of deep guilt and shame.

Alienation and Isolation—Addicts avoid social contact in order to avoid the shame and the embarrassment of having their behavior compared to that of others. There are some who choose to drink alone to avoid feelings of shame. Sooner or later addicts are so unpleasant to be around that their friends avoid them. "Masking" such feelings increases an addict's emotional isolation.

Attempts "To Straighten Out"—Guilt about his drinking along with the vague feeling that he might have a problem are the forces behind an alcoholic's initiating a program of rigorous exercise, health food, physical fitness and good books. Undoing of this sort serves an addict's denial in three ways: it helps him think he has his act together (short of not drinking); it reduces his guilt, and it demonstrates to others and to himself that he doesn't have a problem. Attempts to straighten out include self-denying and even self-punitive measures. Alcoholics have even given up drinking for periods of time to prove they are okay.

Search for a Cure—Eventually an alcoholic's problem becomes apparent even to himself, and he does try to solve it, but he does so without considering drinking the cause and without considering stopping. Over his history, an alcoholic may go to a psychiatrist, psychologist or counselor for help with "personal" problems (not for a drinking problem). He may see a marriage counselor, a family counselor, or a financial counselor. He may change jobs to get a fresh start, or move to a new city, called a "geographic cure." He may seek medical treatments, including tranquilizers for insomnia, anxiety or depression.

The Social Consequences: When a symptom is labeled a "social consequence" of addiction, it does not mean addiction affects one's party life, but that it affects the way he fails to carry out his role as spouse, parent, lover, citizen, worker, employee, student and neighbor.

Symptoms of this sort differ widely with individuals for obvious reasons. Unmarried people do not get divorced due to drinking. Non-drivers are not charged with driving while intoxicated (though they might well be charged with walking while intoxicated if it were an offense). Some alcoholics are fired from jobs, but self-employed alcoholics rarely reprimand themselves for shoddy performance. Though the social consequences differ with individuals, loss of control makes it nearly impossible for an addict to escape every one of these consequences over time.

Family Problems—Separation and divorce—Physical and emotional abuse of spouses, children and parents—Children with emotional problems because of their parent's alcohol and drug problem—Parents with emotional problems because of their children's drug problems—Turmoil at home—Stress from living in an atmosphere tense with powerful and unpredictable emotions—Unexpected and undesirable family relocations.

Relationship Problems—Disturbed love relationships and friendships because of drunkenness and physical abuse—Inability to sustain relationships—Divorce.

Legal Problems—Arrests for drunken driving, disturbing the peace, public intoxication, assault, and disorderly conduct—Law suits resulting from drugged and drug-affected behavior—Jail terms for crimes committed to secure illegal drugs or from using legal ones.

Financial Problems—The cost of alcohol and drugs—Mounting bills because of addiction—Insurance premium increases because of accidents—Extraordinary legal expenses—The costs of repairing or replacing a wrecked automobile, damaged household goods, cigarette-burned clothing.

Household Problems—If the addicted person is the homemaker, the home is likely to be an unhealthy or unsafe environment due to carelessness and neglect. Other problems include burned and wasted food, the expense of buying easy to prepare, more costly foods, and the cost of dining out more than usual.

Job Problems—Absence and lateness—Demotions—Unwanted transfers—Loss of confidence—Conflict with coworkers—Complaints from customers and clients—Damaged reputation—Poor performance—Costly mistakes and errors in judgment—Lost jobs.

School Problems—Lateness, absence, poor grades, cheating, copying homework because an alcoholic student is "too wasted" to do assignments at home are not uncommon for young alcoholics and other addicts. Some are suspended and expelled for drinking and behavioral problems related to it. Reputation as a "head," "burnout," "boozer," "druggie," "drunk," "junkie" is another consequence for young addicts.

The Health Consequences: Two different kinds of health problems result from drug abuse: *direct* damage to the body, such as diseases of the liver; and *indirect* consequences, such as accidents, neglect and secondary illnesses. In an appendix to *Getting Them Sober: Volume III* no fewer than three hundred diseases and disorders are listed as secondary to alcoholism (Drews). The interested reader is referred to this list of potential health symptoms.

There is no way to predict which health problems any individual will suffer, since a number of variables play roles in causing such problems. These variables include the particular drug an individual abuses and the risks associated with that drug, the frequency and amount of its use, the interaction between this drug and other drugs the individual uses, and finally the state of the individual's health and his particular susceptibility to health problems.

Those curious about whether a medical problem is caused or exacerbated by drinking should consult a physician familiar with the diseases and disorders secondary to chemical dependency. One warning, however! If an addict goes to a physician who is not familiar with chemical dependency, or if he lies to his doctor about his drinking and drug use, he may leave the doctor's office with a prescription for a drug which is just as addictive as the one which caused him to go to the doctor in the first place. So many of the health consequences of alcohol or drugs beg for mood altering medication as the antidote that it is quite easy for doctors to consider prescribing them. Anxiety, sleep disturbance, depression, impotence, irritability, mood swings, stomach distress, palpitations, paranoia, high blood pressure, panic attacks, even persistent itching are a few of the health problems caused by alcoholism for which alcoholics have been given addictive substitutes as a remedy.

In addition to the direct harm drugs do to the body, there are indirect consequences—the twin menaces of accidents and neglect. Accidents are common. Addicts fall down stairs, walk into walls and run into cars—both as drivers and pedestrians. Alcoholics have caused explosions, boat crashes and industrial accidents. They have smashed through doors, tumbled out of windows, and fallen off boats. They have stuck their hands into operating machinery and gotten their fingers clipped. They have stuck their noses into other people's business with similar results. Accidents caused by alcoholism would be funny if it were not for the numbers who are maimed and dead because of them, if it were not for the losses to industry and to environments because of them.

Neglect of health is another of addiction's indirect consequences. Teeth rot. Gums swell. Corns harden. Vision blurs. Hearing deteriorates. Eyeglasses and hearing aids are lost and not replaced. Alcohol addicts procrastinate about going to a doctor for so long that a minor problem grows to proportions which require a major medical intervention to correct it. AIDS has been added to the list of addiction's indirect but fatal consequences.

7

The Dynamics of Dependency

Addiction is a movie, not a photograph, a biography, not a portrait. Addiction reads as a story with a beginning, a middle and an end. It is a history in which tolerance, cellular adaptation, growing dependence, symptoms, enablers and denial play interactive roles. Drinking gets worse. Problems get worse. Personalities deteriorate.

Not every story proceeds headlong into destruction. Some alcoholics get sick very slowly and gradually. There are some who can and do stop drinking for periods of time, though eventually they resume, and their drinking gets worse. There are others whose drinking levels out and symptoms abate for periods of time, but addiction is progressive, and sooner or later drinking increases and symptoms intensify.

The Forces of Dependency: Chemical dependency is a complex process with a range of brain and body changes which occur over time, reaching a finale when persistent craving and severe withdrawal are the forces which drive it. But long before that, subtle forces propel it. These forces are threefold. Addictive drinking is cyclic; eventually it is drinking which causes drinking. Next, denial grows thicker with the passing years. Finally, enablers unwittingly help addiction continue.

Knowing the forces which drive addiction provides the clearest clues about how to intervene in the process. As long as an alcoholic drinks, he grows tolerant of alcohol and his brain adapts to a drug in problematic ways. Neither tolerance nor cellular adaptation remit on their own. Only abstinence, achieved either because an addict agrees to try it, or because an authority enforces it, moves addicts toward recovery. An abstinent alcoholic whose brain clears has at least a chance to see he has a problem. Second, denial keeps alcoholics drinking, and so whatever helps denial erode moves in the direction of recovery. Finally, enablers play a part in addiction's progression, and getting enablers to stop enabling aids recovery.

The Nuances of Its Progression: Because addiction happens to all sorts of people, it manifests with a range of individual nuances. No two stories are exactly alike. Alcoholics drink in different ways. Some like "hard stuff"; others prefer beer; and still others wine. Some alcohol addicts drink daily; others on weekends, and a few drink in binges. Every addict has a favorite "drug of choice" and favorite companions, times, and places to go with it.

Individuals experience addiction's symptoms in different ways. For one group addiction progresses from *symptomatic to problematic to compulsive* drug use. In other words, symptoms, such as tolerance and blackouts, are present from the beginning, but neither public problems result from drinking nor is drinking in any obvious way compulsive at the start. Only later does drinking cause problems, and only after that does alcohol become an obsession and its use compulsive. For others the pattern is quite different. For them drinking is compulsive long before it causes problems; it simply grows more compulsive and, therefore, more problematic. And for a third group problems occur right from the start: a drinker charged with driving while intoxicated the very first year he drives a car. Despite the diversity of individuals to whom it happens, the progression of alcoholism is still predictable in its broadest outline.

Three Stages: Chemical Dependency is divided into three stages with specific symptoms marking the transition from one stage to the next. Early alcoholism ends and the middle stage begins when an alcoholic *loses control* and denies it. The middle stage ends and advanced symptoms begin once tolerance has developed and an attempt to stop drinking is followed by binge drinking.

Progressive Symptoms: Certain symptoms appear early on and reappear later, each time worse than before. These are discussed first.

Tolerance

Alcoholics who start out with an early high tolerance for alcohol find, nevertheless, that tolerance still increases and more drug is required to produce a desired effect. Eventually tolerance becomes quite unpredictable, the effect of booze quite variable from one night to the next. One night one-half dozen drinks have no obvious effect, whereas the next night two drinks render the drinker dysfunctional. Finally, tolerance reverses, and small amounts produce disturbing results.

Tolerance is presumed either when the amount someone drinks has to increase if he is to achieve the effect, or when the effect diminishes despite a constant amount. If last year it took four beers and now it takes eight to get a "buzz," that's tolerance. Or if the "buzz" grows fainter and fainter even though the amount remains constant, that's tolerance.

Preoccupation

Preoccupation is another progressive symptom. Alcoholics deny to the very end that they are preoccupied with drinking, but their *looking forward to drinking* becomes *preoccupation,* and *preoccupation finally becomes obsession* provided they live long enough.

Loss of control

Loss of control occurs with increasing frequency and unpredictability over time. At the start alcoholics *lose control* once in a while; later, control slips with greater frequency, and at the end control seems gone entirely. Drunkenness happens so regularly that alcoholics take precautions to insure their safety before setting out to drink. These precautions have been extreme. Alcoholics have locked themselves in motel rooms and mailed their car keys home to avoid endangering themselves while drunk.

Denial and Rationalization: Denial is not only a progressive symptom in alcoholism's history, it is essential to the very process which keeps that history moving. Denial aims not so much at deceiving others as deceiving oneself, and so intelligence is no protection against it. Smart addicts are simply better at denial than stupid ones.

Over time the defenses an alcoholic employs take on a variety of forms. At the beginning an alcoholic minimizes his drinking, problems and feelings. Later he blames others for those problems. Soon he speaks of his drinking in so general a way that any perceptible problem with it evaporates in a mist of words. He disjoints the incidents which make up his history, making each episode seem separate and unconnected. He intellectualizes the problems drinking causes, thereby keeping himself from feeling those problems. He misses the sweep of his symptoms by focusing only on recent ones. He rejects non-drinkers as prudish. He gravitates to people who agree with and collude in his drinking. He distracts himself from his alcoholism by staying angry at all sorts of people for all sorts of reasons. He either finds or invents all sorts of excuses and explanations for his drinking and his problems. He becomes preoccupied with aches and pains so that he has neither the time nor the energy to focus on the effect drinking has on his life. He blocks the truth by fantasizing and regressing. He focuses on peripheral issues in a fine rage: nonsmoking alcoholics lecture eloquently and myopically on the evils of nicotine. In denial an alcoholic is aware of the symptoms he has not manifested more than the ones he has. He jogs, eats nonfat yogurt, goes to church and reads good books—all to demonstrate he has no problem. The result is his disease gets worse.

Early Stage Symptoms: Alcoholism is set on course not because prone individuals drink to escape reality. Ask a dozen alcoholic why they started drinking, and you are likely to get a dozen answers. Most started for the same reasons non-alcoholics started - because it seemed adult, because it was offered, because they heard it made you feel good, because it seemed the time, because it was a way of bonding with peers, because they were shy, because friends drank, and sometimes simply because it was there. But, even though they have no unique reason for starting, alcoholics end up drinking to escape reality. The irony, of course, is that they drink to escape the very reality which drinking created. Early symptoms include:

Blackouts

For some blackouts occur early; others don't black out until the very end; some experience blackouts throughout, and some never black out. When blackouts occur early they are often discounted, thought to be normal, as something which happens to anyone and everyone who drinks.

In our society, joking about blackouts is so common that, partly for that reason, alcoholics consider them insignificant. Only with alcohol is someone likely to dismiss sudden-onset amnesia as funny. If he were to suffer even brief memory lapses because of chocolate milk, he would be off to his doctor frantic for an explanation, and if told to stop drinking chocolate milk altogether, he would. But when he cannot remember an entire evening because of alcohol, he laughs it off. Some day statistics may tell us how common blackouts are among all drinkers. Whatever the truth, when they happen at the start of chemical dependency, denying, minimizing and normalizing them sets a pattern for the future.

Guilt and Shame

When it comes to addiction, guilt has several origins and travels several paths. Alcoholics may feel guilty about drinking itself, sensing from the start that they drink too much or too often. When drunkenness causes foolish, silly or stupid behavior, even ge alcoholics feel the pain. Despite it, however, the drive rink keeps him going to the liquor store regularly, and at some point he feels uneasy about even being seen there. By thirty he is ashamed of neglecting those he loves. And by forty his remorse is poignant when his drunkenness is out of control. Every history has several chapters on guilt.

Tolerance

It is a mistake to think that tolerance is a sign of advanced alcoholism. Some youngsters are tolerant from the start, and it is not uncommon for them to mistake tolerance as freedom from alcoholism, reasoning that if they can hold their booze they won't have a problem. But the alcoholic's problem is not, as the old saw goes, that he cannot hold his booze. His problem is that he can hold it—and much too much of it.

Drifting Toward Other Addicts

Drinkers gravitate to drinkers. Addicts find addicts. The process begins early, and the reasons are multiple. One individual's heavy drinking is easily masked in a room where everyone is a heavy drinker. Alcoholics who surround themselves with alcoholics find it easy to see their own drinking as normal. In a "world" of alcoholics, alcoholic drinking is the norm. There will always be a good supply in a room of heavy drinkers.

From Early to Middle Stage: When a drinker repeatedly explains away his drunkenness and his *loss of control,* and when he blames others for the problems which result from his drinking, addiction moves to a more serious stage, and intervention by an outside agent becomes increasingly necessary to halt it. An alcoholic who believes he is not sick is powerless to stop being sick. Symptoms intensify.

Middle Stage: In the middle stage of the disease, an alcoholic's inability to control his drinking occurs with increased frequency. Family, job, marital and legal problems begin, increase or intensify. Addicts get sick emotionally. Their reasoning grows convoluted.

With denial in place, an alcoholic blames almost anything but his own loss of control for his drunkenness. If he cannot blame others he will be forced to see *loss of control* as the cause of his drunking, and that conclusion is unacceptable. Parental neglect and indifference, stressful jobs, disappointments in love, too strict an upbringing, early repressive religious education come in for a fair share of the blame as well.

Extravagance

Alcoholics, as they get sicker, are forced into proving to themselves and others that they are neither sick nor bad. This "proof" may take the form of acts of generosity, sometimes quite extravagant. Alcoholics give of their time, money, and advice, unaware that part of their motivation is to prove they are not alcoholic. Christmas provides a perfect opportunity for an alcoholic to put on a display of opulence for his family. Giving lavish gifts and treating the family to an unexpected and expensive winter vacation helps him believe he is not in trouble with booze while providing him a reason to reward himself for being a good fellow - with a drink, of course. Alcoholism goes rampant at Christmas for reasons other than the general acceptability of drinking at that season. Addiction takes whatever opportunity life offers "to let her rip," and Christmas offers such opportunity. The structure of the workweek keeps addiction in check, but on weekends and holidays drinking runs rampant. A summer vacation provides an opportunity for excess. A promotion is a good excuse to get plastered. A demotion serves equally as well. Alcoholics are magicians; they can turn anything into a drink.

The Role Resentment Plays

From the start Alcoholics Anonymous recognized that resentment plays a major role in relapse, that by harboring resentments alcoholics shut themselves off from recovery and drink again (*Alcoholics Anonymous,* pp. 64-66). Vernon Johnson, an early treatment practitioner, recognized that chemical dependency does more than trigger resentments; it creates the "more chronic condition of having become a resentful person," and he recognized that without treatment, resentfulness would "drive the patient back into the bottle" (Johnson, pp. 78-79).

As addiction progresses, in part because his brain is poisoned, resentments become persistent and obsessional. Angry feelings about past injustice, abuse or neglect, real or trumped up, are resurrected and re-felt. To the casual observer, harping on old resentments indicates an alcoholic has personality problems, but the truth is that alcoholics harbor resentments because they are useful to them as alcoholics. Resentment is not coincidental to alcoholism; the role it plays is dynamic and twofold. First, resentments provide alcoholics with an explanation for why their lives are going badly. Without implicating their drinking they blame present circumstances on past injustices and harms. Resentments also provide an excuse to drink. When he can find no other reason, resentments provide an alcoholic with a ready-made justification. "You'd drink too if you had a wife or a life like mine." Addiction is efficient; it wastes little energy; it uses whatever life puts at its disposal. With remarkable facility, addiction turns even justified, preexisting resentments into playing a chemical dependency role.

The dynamic relationship of resentment to active disease becomes apparent in recovery. Once he quits drinking, his head clears, and he accepts that drinking causes him problems, an alcoholic's resentments no longer serve a purpose, and in many cases resentments dissipate. Resentments which have been harbored for years have been known to disappear with no more treatment than abstinence. True, there are alcoholics for whom resentfulness has become so ingrained that extra help from an AA sponsor or professional familiar with recovery is helpful to avoid the thin ice of early recovery. And there are and probably always will be addicts for whom resentfulness was present and disruptive in their lives before addiction became a problem, and additional therapy may be necessary for them once they are sober. Finally, there are recovering alcoholics who find that the conditions which foster resentment persist into recovery. An alcoholic whose family remains distant, controlling, bitter and mistrustful years after he has been sober may find that additional support and counseling are helpful in handling resentments which if ignored can create the conditions for relapse.

Hiding Use

Eventually an alcoholic realizes he wants more booze than even he believes appropriate, and then he must become secretive about it. Sneaking into a bathroom to drink from a bottle hidden in a linen closet is one way of doing this. Pouring six ounces of booze into a glass and calling it a single drink is another. Drinking before arriving at a party is a third. Not all alcoholics hide bottles. Many do hide how much and how often they drink.

Control Ploys

Eventually only the most intractable alcoholic will fail to realize he gets drunker than he intends and will make some effort to "limit" his drinking. What motivates such control ploys is that *loss of control* threatens to break through denial and into consciousness. Instead, he convinces himself that his excesses are of recent vintage and a matter of mere carelessness - that all he has to do is get these recent lapses under control. And so, even as he establishes ploys to control his drinking, his denial keeps him from realizing why he must.

Control ploys are not intended to keep an alcoholic from drinking; they are meant to keep him from getting "too" drunk. What follows are familiar ploys with that purpose in mind. The list is worded with alcoholics, street and prescription addicts in mind. The ploys are occasionally funny; at times they are just plain astonishing.

- Switching from hard liquor to beer or wine.
- Switching to light beer.
- Switching brands of liquor or types of drug.
- Switching to a lower proof or a less potent drug.
- Postponing drinking until after dinner.
- Prolonging the interval between doses.

- Changing the times and places one drinks.
- Changing drinking companions.
- Carefully measuring drinks in a graded tumbler.
- Trying to skip a dose or a day.
- Going clean for the weekend.
- Keeping a careful written record of drinks or doses.
- Buying a fixed amount to limit use in that way.
- Refrigerating a fixed number of beers to limit use.
- Drinking / using only on weekends.
- Drinking / using only after noon.
- Alternating alcoholic with non-alcoholic drinks.
- Alternating more potent with less potent drugs.
- Keeping alcohol in inconvenient places so that it's hard to get.
- Trying to stick to weak drinks or mild drugs.
- Eating a full meal before drinking.
- Limiting the money one takes when he goes out.
- Supplementing alcohol with another drug.
- Stopping for a period of time to regain health.

One alcoholic kept booze in the trunk of his car to make drinking inconvenient and thereby limit how much he drank. In the dead of winter he would have to put on his overcoat, go to the car, open the trunk, get the bottle, bring it inside, pour a drink, return the bottle to the trunk, and go back inside. Before the evening was over, either the bottle found its way inside, or he found himself curbside. Another alcoholic switched from home drinking to bar drinking, reasoning that bar drinks would be too expensive and thus limit how much he drank. Later he switched to home drinking, blaming the bar's atmosphere for encouraging excess. He got as drunk in an easy chair as on a barstool. A third alcoholic changed drinking companions, blaming his buddies for getting him wasted only to find he got as wasted with new friends—and even all alone. One alcoholic, in a familiar ploy, drank beer on weeknights, reserving hard liquor for the weekends so he would not be too hung over to go to work. Another (there are probably many) switched from bourbon to scotch because he had convinced himself that there was a particular ingredient in bourbon which made him mean. He was right. He found the same ingredient in scotch, chablis, vodka, and malt liquor. A high school student who was hospitalized by the time she was eighteen limited herself to three dollars whenever she went bar drinking, believing she would go home after her three dollars were spent. By day she was a good student, a better than average athlete, and well liked by her peers. By night she hustled male customers for drinks after her three dollars had been spent. She ended the evening vomiting. It was routine.

A prescription addict discovered he was too drugged to function in the middle of the day and so skipped his noon dose only to take double or triple doses at dinnertime. And countless are the addicts who increase their marijuana consumption as a way to cut down on another drug which has gotten out of hand. Over the long haul, control ploys fail. Using them, however, deceives one into thinking he is in control.

Seeking "Other" Help

With a family in turmoil, job performance deteriorating, alternating fits of depression and aggression, mounting debts, and a marriage (pardon the expression) "on the rocks," an alcoholic may realize he needs help of some kind. And eventually he does seek help, but not to stop drinking. In fact, if he goes to a doctor who confronts him about his drinking, he will find another doctor. Alcoholics have seen psychiatrists, counselors, surgeons, physicians, nurses, family therapists, psychologists, marriage counselors, priests, social workers, financial counselors, ministers, sex therapists and good friends looking for help to solve alcoholism's symptoms without addressing their cause.

Doctors find it easier to ask probing questions in search of a diagnosis of alcoholism if they perceive their inquiries as uncovering symptoms, not as revealing shame. Sadly, however, health professionals in a position to help alcoholics either do not ask, do not know how to ask, or feel uncomfortable asking questions which will help an alcoholic focus on his problem. Regardless, the professional who does confront an addict ought to be prepared to deal with anger, denial and evasion. In the thick of his disease an alcoholic does not want to be treated for it. He wants its consequences to go away.

Anxiety About Supply

Addicts feel anxious about whether they have bought enough, afraid they will run out. Drinking, drugging and getting the "stuff" become full time jobs. Three flakes of snow fall, and alcoholics are off to liquor stores apprehensive about facing a coming blizzard without a stock. After she had snorted a single line of cocaine, an addicted professional was certain she should have bought two grams instead of one. Bulk buying for addicts is not a matter of economics.

From Middle to Late Stage: Having progressed through the middle stage of an addiction, even a headstrong alcoholic realizes he needs to slow down, stop for a while, or quit drinking altogether. When unrelieved drinking, called a binge, follows a period of self-imposed abstinence, addiction moves to its final stage. If tolerance has developed, drinking after a dry spell picks up as if it had to make up for lost time, as if some preset level of drug had to be regained. The appetite is ravenous.

Late Stage Symptoms: The word, "addict" comes from a Latin word which the Romans used when referring to the sentence given a *captured* enemy. Whoever chose it to describe drug dependence must have known addiction's final stage. At that stage an addict is captive, his symptoms extreme. Drunkenness is frequent, outrageous, rageful. At this stage alcoholics can become homicidal or suicidal. Drunkenness is followed by abject guilt and shame. Attempts at control fail miserably. When dry, he is obsessed with alcohol. At this point an alcoholic no longer drinks for fun; he drinks to escape. Day in and day out he is depressed, guilt-ridden, drugged, agitated and withdrawing. Cycles of drinking and withdrawing are vicious. Health deteriorates. Medical emergencies crop up. Catastrophe is imminent.

The fears alcoholics experience at this stage are unreal, bizarre. One alcoholic feared that his children would fall out of a window. His was fear so vivid that he would grab any of his children who walked near a window. Another convinced himself that snakes had gotten into the plumbing of his house. It made going to the bathroom difficult. Such fears have been known to simply disappear with abstinence but losing the fear seems unlikely to those in the throes of alcoholism.

At the final stage alcoholics find it hard to imagine living without alcohol. Some resign themselves to drinking; others convince themselves they are not addicted even after bouts of alcoholic hallucinosis. The layman is certain one would have to be crazy not to see the truth at this stage. Such reasoning is not far from the truth.

Cycles of Symptoms: Symptoms not only follow each other in a string. Early symptoms precipitate later drinking, and the two, symptoms and drinking, form a circle in which drinking relieves symptoms which drinking caused. Addiction breeds resentfulness, and resentments become an excuse to drink. Friday's drinking causes Saturday morning's irritability, and Saturday evening's drinking soothes it. Drinking aims to relieve the very depression it has caused. Drinking drives friends away; alcohol fills the void. Alcohol makes one nervous and sleepless, and then it is used as tranquilizer and sleeping pill. The list goes on. The most obvious cycle in which a drug relieves the problem it has caused is withdrawal. But long before withdrawal, cycles of symptoms push addiction along its progressive course.

At What Point Sick? At some point it is no longer reasonable to think of a problem drinker as merely troubled; he is "sick." When Dr. Vaillant says alcoholism *be-*

comes a disease when loss of control causes an individual's morbidity (p. 44), what he means is not that drinking alcohol makes someone dependent on it, but that alcoholism is not called a "disease" until loss of control causes problems. But are alcoholics "sick" before drinking causes "recurring" problems? Can an adolescent be called sick with "addiction" before drinking completely wrecks his life?

Loss of control—that one after another chain of drinks, once it is established as a pattern, might be one point at which to call alcoholism a "disease," but *loss of control* occurs so early in some cases that it seems premature to say that someone who has exhibited even repeated instances of *loss of control* without other consequences is as sick as someone who has lost his job and part of his liver because of it. *Loss of control* occurs too early in some cases to claim that it is the "disease" stage. There is another point which happens after *loss of control* but before morbid consequences, a point at which one's drug involvement is more serious than a mere habit and a potential problem. That point occurs when the drinking-symptom-drinking cycle meets *loss of control*, and both are denied. At that point a drinker reaches a critical juncture in his history. His drinking self perpetuates. It is unpredictable. He can see neither. At this point the drinker cannot solve his problem because he does not see he has one. *He is* the problem. He is trapped. He can only get worse. He may not seek treatment for his condition until it causes recurring problems, but when *loss of control* is a given, when *drinking breeds drinking*, and when denial blocks one from seeing both, then morbid consequences are not merely probable, they are inevitable.

Whether addicts reach this point because of their brain's chemistry and its response to drugs, or because they perceive drugs as pleasurable, or by some combination of chemistry, perception and memory, addicts are sick from the moment *loss of control*, cyclic drinking and denial form a partnership.

The Dynamic Role of Enabling: Enabling is the other force which moves addiction along. Find an addict, and you will find four, five, six or more people who enable his addiction to continue. To remain active, an alcoholic must have help. He may need look no farther than his own living room, but he will need help to cover up the consequences of his drinking, to deny it is a problem, and to patch up the troubles it causes. Those who badger him will find they provide him an excuse to drink when he runs out of his own excuses. Enabling takes the form of people, places, and things.

Enabling People: Because enabling serves a variety of purposes, family members are naturals for the job. They are close at hand and have a vested interest, and so quite understandably husbands and wives, mothers and fathers, sons and daughters end up enabling, believing all the while that what they are doing is the loving, the right and even the helpful thing.

One need not volunteer for the job of enabler to get it. If an enabler is not nearby, addicts seek them out. Some enablers play the role willingly, and others are suckered into it. Some addicts do enjoy "conning" others into enabling them, but not all addicts are con artists by inclination. Addiction coerces even those who are unwilling into manipulating others to act as enablers. Bosses, doctors, policemen, counselors, lawyers, neighbors and co-workers have been duped into it, unaware that it has happened.

Circumstances as Enabling: Circumstances can enable an addict. A steady flow of cash helps an addict continue to use drugs. The one clear difference between a rich addict and a poor one is that the rich one can afford to stay sicker longer.

Jobs that do not require a strict accounting of a worker's time and productivity help alcoholics to get away with drinking without apparent problems. Businesses that sanction their employees drinking with clients enable those employees who are alcoholic. Alcoholic teachers do get away with inadequate preparation and poor classroom performance. Lawyers, outside salesmen, any worker who sets his own schedule can keep mornings free to recover from nights before, and thus their jobs enable their alcoholism. An alcoholic bartender is in heaven, as is a drug dependent pharmacist—both in the midst of a virtually limitless supply. Jobs do not cause alcoholism; they enable it.

Places do not cause alcoholism; neighborhoods do not cause it. However, alcoholics and other addicts are drawn to certain places, neighborhoods and scenes because excessive drinking and drugging are permitted, common, even expected there. For sure, certain vacation resorts are popular with alcoholics because they provide a no limits atmosphere in which to practice excess with impunity, as if the laws of the normal world were suspended at seaside resorts. Every city has neighborhoods which are not breeding grounds for addiction as much as they are places where addicts end up—places which attract and hold addicts because they supply, mask and enable addiction.

Put simply, enabling prolongs alcoholism by helping an alcoholic delay either hitting bottom or feeling it. Someone who has been acting in an enabling way can help an alcoholic by stopping.

Hitting Bottom: Believing an alcoholic must "hit bottom" before he recovers is a truth expressed in unfortunately extreme language. "Bottom" is imagined in such extreme ways that there are very few addicts who will last long enough to reach it in this life. Years ago alcoholics stayed sick longer than they had to. Today, intervention is the practice by which concerned others ban together with experts to cut short active addiction by presenting the addict a vivid picture of his condition and offering treatment for it. Contemporary thinking holds that denial causes alcoholics to be unable to recognize that he has bottomed out. So, someone will have to pick "bottom" up and hit him with it.

Bottom is not an event; it is not a situation; it is not a set of words; and it is not a physical condition. It is an awareness. An alcoholic hits bottom not when he says, "I am alcoholic," not even when he considers his a particularly bad case. Alcoholics do continue to drink long after both.

Denial keeps addicts from feeling the pain of their drinking and its consequences, and pain *is* part of what hitting bottom is about. And so, when denial erodes enough so that drinking hurts, then bottom is near. But pain itself is not bottom. Bottom happens when an addict utters one four-letter word, **"HELP."** Addiction humiliates its victim. Bottom occurs when it humbles him, when he becomes teachable, when he asks for help. To ask for help means that one must stop dictating the form which that help takes. An alcoholic who asks for help but who then continues to make decisions contrary to the advice he is offered, who controls the source and course of his help is far from bottom. He is like the ocean voyager who is washed overboard and when thrown an orange life preserver asks for a choice of color. To hit bottom is to feel powerless. It is to ask for help unconditionally. It is to surrender.

8

Early Recovery

By 1968, the American Medical Association had already defined alcoholism as an illness characterized by a "tendency to relapse" (p. 6). Recovery does not always begin the first time an alcoholic stops drinking because the forces at work in early abstinence so characteristically retrigger drinking or lead to other drug use that early abstinence itself is best viewed as part of the active disease and integral to its process.

Designed to Destroy: Viewed anthropomorphically, addiction is intent on destroying its victim. It makes him sick. It tells him he's not sick. And after he does stop drinking, it makes him feel worse before he feels better.

It may seem silly to call alcoholism a killer because it makes one sick; lots of other diseases do that. Few, however, do as thorough a job. Alcoholism makes an alcoholic sick in a thoroughgoing way: physically, mentally and emotionally. But unlike other diseases, denial prevents an alcoholic from seeing that he is sick. The result is that he continues to drink and gets sicker. But there is more. Once he stops drinking, the shock of three withdrawals greets him: acute withdrawal, post-acute withdrawal, and a third withdrawal which might be called "psychological." He suffers emotional pain, which he must handle without resorting to drugs for relief. His problems feel overwhelming. His brain is stressed from years of abuse. And all this sets him up to drink. And if he does drink, his disease resumes; he gets sicker, denies it more vigorously, and after several bouts of relapse, surrenders to the drug with greater despair than ever before. The simple truth is that some simply do not stay sober *through* early recovery precisely *because of* it.

Three Withdrawals: Recovery confronts the novice with a series of shocks. First, there is acute withdrawal, a relatively brief period during which particular mood altering drugs, if stopped abruptly, cause a disturbing physical reaction in those who have become dependent on them. In extreme cases with particular drugs, withdrawal can be life threatening. Acute withdrawal is followed by a period during which newly sober alcoholics continue to be at the mercy of a nervous system which has taken a beating for years and is likely to remain unstable for a time. This is post acute withdrawal. Finally, there is a series of shocks, described metaphorically as "psychological withdrawal." This three-part continuum is early recovery. For a few it is short-lived and comparatively mild. For many it seems intense and eternal. For some it's a killer.

Acute Withdrawal: An addict who is dependent on a drug must maintain a level of the drug if his nervous system is to remain stable. Should he abruptly stop his drug, he will experience a kind of "shock." When that shock is measurable, it is called "acute withdrawal." If his drug is a sedative, withdrawal will take the form of a hyper-stimulated nervous system, causing vital signs, blood pressure, temperature and pulse rate to rise. If he has been using a stimulant drug, cocaine or amphetamine for example, withdrawal will take the form of a crash—with lethargy, fatigue, muscular aches and pains, and depression sometimes severe enough to precipitate suicide (Schuckit 1984a, pp. 97-98).

Withdrawal from alcohol begins within twenty-four hours after a last drink and peaks within two to three days with measurable signs lasting four to five days (Schuckit 1984a, pp. 74-75). Withdrawal from minor tranquilizers and barbiturates begins within twelve hours but may not fully emerge until the seventh day after abstinence, and some symptoms last for quite a long time (Schuckit 1984a, pp. 34-36). Symptoms of sedative withdrawal run the spectrum from anxiety, restlessness, palpitations, hot and cold sweats, sleep disturbances and "shakes" to convulsions, hallucinations, and the most serious and a life-threatening complication of alcohol withdrawal, delirium tremens.

The cycle of drug use—withdrawal—drug use is easy to guess. The more an alcoholic drinks, the more intense his withdrawal. The more intense his withdrawal, the more he drinks to relieve it. And the more he drinks to relieve it, the more he suffers withdrawal next time he stops, and the more he reacts in ways which cause even more stress. Of course the more stressed he is, the more he drinks.

Withdrawal does not appear overnight, out of the blue. An alcoholic is not fine one day and in acute withdrawal the next. The insidiousness of withdrawal is that many contend with its subtler symptoms for months without knowing it. And since withdrawal invites the sufferer to take the very drug which produces it, alcoholics self medicate, using alcohol or a "freeze dried" substitute, a tranquilizer, to soothe withdrawal symptoms.

In acute withdrawal an alcoholic is neither a pleasant nor a welcome sight. And if the only time one has contact with him is when he is withdrawing, smelling of booze, arrogant, shaky and demanding, he seems entirely despicable, incredibly imperceptive—one of a stupid lot of people. Compassion is possible only if one appreciates the long and fitful history that brought him to that point, though admittedly at that point he is still not cuddly.

Post-Acute Withdrawal: Once acute withdrawal ends, the danger of convulsions and life-threatening complications ends. Withdrawal, however, does not end. There is a second period awaiting the newcomer, a period overcast with uncertainty and punctuated by sudden emotional storms. This is post acute withdrawal. It has not been well studied, its causes and duration have yet to be defined with precision, and so skeptics find it difficult to accept post acute withdrawal as anything more than the exaggeration of a stressed imagination. Recovering addicts, however, tell stories about early recovery which are so similar, despite the fact that they come from very different story tellers, that post acute withdrawal seems more reasonably attributed to physical rather than psychological forces.

Unfortunately there is no data-supported answer to the question which Al-Anon spouses most often ask, "How long does this damned early recovery stuff last?" Alcoholics Anonymous tells new members that they are too sick to make any major changes in their lives for a "year," but post acute withdrawal is rarely used as the name for that year. The advice most often passed on to AA newcomers is to "keep coming back; it gets better." One of the hopes AA offers is that early recovery is endurable. Veterans laugh at how they agonized and analyzed those days. To the rookie it isn't funny.

Agitation and Restlessness

During acute withdrawal an individual may experience so much motor restlessness and agitation that he must pace back and forth to relieve it. Even after acute withdrawal, he may feel agitated and anxious, but this decreases in frequency and intensity in time.

Aches and Pains

Nonspecific aches and pains should not shock someone who has been drinking heavily and steadily for years. He can expect them. If those aches and pains are specifically focused, if they are severe, or if they persist and increase, the newcomer should consult a doctor who can figure out the cause and recommend a solution, but he should seek a physician committed to avoiding mood-altering drugs for chemically dependent people. An alcoholic is responsible for his recovery and must take steps to insure he does not deceive himself or his physicians into thinking he needs psychoactive drugs. An AA friend or a sponsor can help him stay honest with himself. Self-honesty is critical throughout recovery but especially in its early days.

Anxiety Attacks

One of the many problems of post acute withdrawal and one of the most disconcerting, is its sudden attack of anxiety—anxiety which comes on for no apparent reason or for reasons which are moderate compared to the anxiety they provoke. Anxiety prompts someone newly sober to believe that tranquilizers are their remedy, and even well meaning physicians can be persuaded into prescribing them for alcoholics in distress. There are several pathways to a prescription addiction in early recovery.

"Bad Chemistry Days"

Not a very scientific name but a very common experience, "bad chemistry days" are those days when newly dry alcoholics awaken agitated. No sooner has he opened his eyes than he feels shaky, disturbed and convinced something is sure to go wrong. Here's how one alcoholic expressed his bewilderment and frustration with the experience. "I figured something must be wrong with me. I'd wake up irritated even though nothing had yet happened. It was too damned early in the day for anything to have gone wrong, and yet I'd be ready to pick a fight."

The researcher who compiles a list of the types and duration of what are "normal" problems in early recovery will do splendid service for recovering alcoholics who are comforted to learn that the problems which bother them are a familiar part of early recovery. If hard evidence backed that up, newcomers could approach early recovery with the confidence that there are certain problems which are an expected part of getting well, and not a sign of getting worse. Such data would also provide treating professionals with guidelines for determining when an individual's problems are beyond the expertise of self-help.

Diminished Concentration

A frustrating experience, especially for those whose jobs require attention to detail, is that powers of concentration are diminished in early recovery and remain so for a while.

Return of Dreaming

One surprise for those whose drug use has robbed them of normal sleep is that dreaming returns. Rebound dreaming is nearly always vivid and memorable. Some dreams are pleasant; some unsettling; some are nightmares. Dreaming about drinking and drug use is not uncommon. Addicts dream about what they have loved and lost.

"Dry Drunks"

Though its exact cause is unknown, the "dry drunk" is a familiar phenomenon. "Dry drunk" means that the physical condition is "dry," but the behavior is *like* a drunk's, not literally staggering and slurring, but like a drinker's emotions—demanding, moody, arrogant, agitated, depressed. Dry drunks leave as quickly as they come, but these behaviors frighten family members who wonder whether they mean that drinking has resumed. They put additional stress on already strained relationships.

Emotional Augmentation

The protracted withdrawal syndrome described in *Under The Influence* includes increased emotional hypersensitivity (Milam, pp. 66-67, 97-98). The problem persists in early recovery. Emotional reactions exceed the stimuli which trigger them.

Flashes of Fear

Someone sober for the first time in years may experience spasms of fear, such as a child's fear of the dark, or a brief fit of fear of driving. These attacks are not usually debilitating. They last usually only a short time, and nearly everyone functions throughout, unsettling though these fears may be.

Fogged Thinking

Recovering addicts remain in a "fog" for a time, and nothing makes that clearer than coming out of it. Addiction progresses so gradually that it is like living in a world which has been overcast for so long that one forgets what the sun looks like. And so, when the sun shines, it's a surprise.

Hypersensitivity and Self Consciousness

"Emotionally touchy" describes a newcomer. Along with emotional hypersensitivity comes painful self-consciousness. They make quite a pair.

Memory Problems

Short-term memory deficits are part of early recovery. For some, the deficit is permanent, and individuals learn to compensate. Poor memory is exasperating and can be a source for anxiety about future functioning. An already sick mind finds it easy to rationalize poor memory as indicating a damaged brain and a hopeless recovery. And thinking like that easily provides an excuse to return to booze.

Itching

Itching during acute withdrawal, which old timers refer to as "whiskey fleas," plagues a few.

Mood Swings

Though not nearly as extreme as the mood swings experienced by those with bipolar (manic-depressive) disorder, fluctuations of mood are part of early recovery. To someone who is sensitive to the novelty of feeling at all, mood swings seem intense, and newcomers think that medication may be needed to control them. Early recovery mood lability levels out with time. Again, if mood swings persist or increase, an individual should consult a psychiatrist familiar with the differences between early recovery mood lability, bipolar mood swings, and depression's cycling.

Obsessive Ruminating

Ruminative thinking about trivial matters plagues early recovery for some. Addicts wonder if they are about to make a stupid mistake and find they check and recheck to prevent it.

The thoughts are almost obsessive. One common obsessive thought, one complicated by poor memory, is that something has been forgotten, left undone, unattended.

Limited Attention Span

There is little wonder Alcoholics Anonymous publishes short, easy-to-read pamphlets available to the newcomer. Attention span and powers of concentration are limited.

Sleep Difficulties

A recovering alcoholic may not sleep normally for as many as five months after becoming abstinent. Many sleep fitfully. They fall asleep quickly but awaken in the middle of the night fully alert. Or they do not fall asleep until early morning and then awaken an hour later, fatigued. If sleep disturbances persist beyond five months or so, an alcoholic should consult a professional familiar with early recovery to determine if something else is causing a sleep problem. Other fairly common reasons alcoholics have trouble sleeping is that they consume too much caffeine and nicotine before bedtime, and they ruminate over unresolved shame, guilt and resentment. The biggest danger is that early recovery sleep problems will be treated with sleeping pills.

The Third Withdrawal: After the first two withdrawals, there is a third which is no less troublesome and no less jeopardizing to sobriety. When he stops drinking, an alcoholic eliminates not only a drug which has kept his brain in balance, he also eliminates a drug which provided activity, pleasure, companionship, structure and meaning. When the fog lifts, there is a third shock, a psychological one. Whether the problems of early recovery are caused by chemistry or psychology is academic. To the sufferer both are equally distressing.

Grief

Addicts love drugs. Even when they do not like the taste or the ambience which surrounds the drinking of it, alcoholics love the feeling they get from alcohol. Addiction is a lot like love. Love is blind; denial is a sort of blindness. Addicts have trouble believing drugs are his problem; lovers have trouble accepting their loved ones have faults. The analogy becomes apparent in recovery when an alcoholic spends his lunch hour drinking tonic water and socializing with buddies in bars. He is like the boy whose girl friend has dropped him but who drives past her house on his way home.

Because addiction is like love, recovery is like grief—similar to the feelings experienced by those who have lost a loved one (cf. Kubler-Ross, pp. 100-101): *shock* - that one is alcoholic; *guilt*—about the past; *loneliness—a sense of isolation*—resulting from the loss of friends; *fear*—that one will not be able to handle the demands of recovery, and *anger and resentment*—about being alcoholic and having to deal with recovery. Ultimately, an alcoholic finds acceptance but not at the beginning.

Awakening to Consequences

To awaken from addiction is to awaken to its consequences, a lifetime of them: damage to health, injury to family, harm to career, havoc wreaked on self esteem and confidence, the erosion of structure and meaning in life. It's painful.

Continuing Struggles with Denial

Proficiency at self-deception does not evaporate the day someone gets sober. After the first battle with denial, comes a second set of skirmishes. It is common for alcoholics in early abstinence to wonder whether they are "really" alcoholic. "Did I really lose control? Could I have controlled my drinking if I had tried harder—*really* tried? I might have exaggerated my problem; I was in such bad shape I might have been vulnerable to thinking I had a problem when I didn't." For some alcoholics the only evidence which quiets such doubts is to experiment with "controlled" drinking. Unfortunately, some take long journeys back into drinking and drugging and denying. Some never return.

Drinking Dreams

Addicts who stop taking drugs dream about them. Alcoholics drink; nicotine addicts smoke; cocaine addicts snort, and heroin addicts inject in their dreams. The dreams are memorable and nearly always in Technicolor, but they are neither universally pleasant nor frightening. A Freudian interpretation is likely to regard such dreams as wish fulfillment or expression of subconscious anxiety. A simpler explanation is that the dreamer is an addict twenty-four hours a day, even as he sleeps.

Identity and Purpose of Life

After coming out of the fog, alcoholics, especially those who got started on drinking in their early teens, begin asking questions the fog has deferred. "Who am I? What do I enjoy?" "How will I relax?" "Am I shy? "How will I have fun?" "What's life about?" One newly recovering alcoholic expressed his early recovery philosophizing this way. "I sat in a mall on a Saturday afternoon watching people shop and imagined they were buying clothes for work the next week, all the while thinking that they were going to work so that they could make money to come back the following weekend to buy even more clothes for the week after. Is that what non-alcoholics do with their lives?" Is that life? Another alcoholic, one of many, discovered that he enjoyed certain forms of recreation simply because drinking was part of them. In recovery he didn't especially enjoy big league baseball and wasn't crazy about loud parties.

For someone who has never been addicted, it is difficult to appreciate how central drinking can become for an alcoholic. When he says drinking is the only thing he does for himself, it is only barely overstatement. In fact, as dependency worsens, even those alcoholics who used to enjoy their jobs find their attitudes change. The job provides little satisfaction in itself. It is a means to an end. That end is to drink. And so to lose drinking is to lose one's reason for working. It is not surprising sober alcoholics begin to wonder if they should change jobs or start new careers.

Inhibition and Self Consciousness

AA members sooner or later recognize that they waste part of every AA meeting rehearsing what to say if called on. Drunks get lots of practice spouting insights in uninhibited, free form style when loaded, but they have had little practice saying what they think and feel sober. Recovery is a self-conscious time. When alcohol or other drugs have been part of sex, sober lovemaking is awkward and embarrassing, clumsy and inept, and, for a few, impossible for a time. One of the quickest roads back to drinking is paved with the thought that sobriety means no more of the joy of sex.

The Shock of Feelings

For an addict who has not weathered an emotional experience without a drug, sober feelings jolt when they hit. Mild feelings seem strong; powerful feelings astonish, and augmented ones overwhelm. In early recovery feelings are accompanied by two messages. "Feelings are overwhelming. They are everlasting." They seem remorseless and relentless. Guilt, anger, anxiety, resentment, fear, sadness, hurt, shame and loneliness come in extra helpings, and they come augmented and intensified. Even love, peace and happiness feel peculiar. For an emotional beginner joy seems strange, and it may bring tears. Alcoholism never taught anyone to feel normally.

The Insidiousness of Early Recovery: Early recovery is filled with ironies. Alcoholism takes away one's ability to deal with stress and then gives one more stress to deal with. Alcohol blurs reality, and reality comes blaring back in recovery—a reality made more painful than it is for others because of addiction, and a reality which must be endured without chemical relief, without tranquilizers. Alcoholism robs one of the opportunities to learn about feelings, and then dishes up extra helpings of feelings to be experienced undrugged for the first time in years, feelings intensified by an agitated nervous system. Recovering alcoholics know well that they may never drink again, and yet the world seems intent on reminding them that "weekends are made for Michelob."

Getting Through Early Recovery: If there is a goal for early recovery, it is to get through it. How? Any way that works! Why? To save your ass. Faced with the question of how one will save his life, there ought to be little interest in programs aimed at achieving personal fulfillment and potential through intellectual stimulation and emotional discovery.

> The object is to learn how not to drink.
> The motive is to stay alive.
> And the method is any one which will work.

The wisest move an alcoholic or other drug addict can make is to go to Alcoholics and/or Narcotics Anonymous, and the reasons are simple. It's free. It's available. It works. Faced with nearly any other problem, individuals do not choose solutions which are expensive, hard to access and unreliable. They pick something which is inexpensive, dependable, and easy to get to. But when alcoholism is the problem and Alcoholics Anonymous is suggested as the solution, otherwise sane people ask if there isn't another way. The reason for so perverse a stance reduces quite often to two deeply human truths: pride and denial. To go to Alcoholics Anonymous is to admit *you need help to stop drinking*. After all, only *real* alcoholics go to AA.

The newcomer who goes to AA finds people whose interest is to stay sober and help others do the same—people who accomplish the former by the latter. When he finds sober AA members, he finds no critics, no judges and no experts. He hears no mandates, no rules, no regulations, and no edicts. He sees no bosses, no chain of command and no organizational superstructure. He meets people—some pleasant and some unpleasant, some young and some old, some preachy and some tolerant, some brilliant and some not, some shy, some talkative, some extroverted, some like him and others not, some who are sicker than others. He finds people helping each other.

9

ADDICTION

Learning about addiction is impossible as long as one presumes that depictions of it on television and in the movies are typical. The lives of addicts are not as exciting as prime time would lead us to believe. Some live dangerously of course, but most suffer with less excitement than the big screen shows. Alcoholics are drug addicts. Rarely, however, are they called so. Initially, therefore, learning about addiction involves unlearning one's preconceptions about it.

Extreme Images: A young woman who used every drug available to her on the streets and most of those found in pharmacies, and who put those drugs into her body by nearly every orifice available, refused to call herself a drug addict because she had never injected heroin. To her that was real addiction, and as with many addicts who want to think of addiction as extreme behavior, she hadn't done that. It helped her to deny she had the problem.

Alcoholics generally do not regard themselves as drug addicts for several reasons, not the least of which is their failure to perceive alcohol as a drug. Crystal decanters and cocktail shakers have been drug paraphernalia in this country for a lot longer than pot bongs and coke spoons, and yet alcoholics use "addict," to refer to the "hard core." Even that phrase, "hard core," when it refers to heroin addicts, reflects a use of language with little basis in either logic or common sense. By any criteria for determining how dangerous a drug happens to be, alcohol should be considered more troublesome than heroin because it is more toxic and because withdrawal from it can be life-threatening, whereas heroin withdrawal, though distressing and protracted, is not. Heroin addicts die in withdrawal but not from of it. They die of overdose; they commit suicide; they are murdered, or die in accidents. They do not, however, die as the direct medical consequence of heroin withdrawal. As consequences go, death from alcohol withdrawal seems more profound than diarrhea from heroin withdrawal, and yet heroin is called the "hard" drug, and alcohol, if called a drug at all, is a "soft" one.

Old ideas die hard. Americans equate addiction not only with particular drugs and particular means of using them. Two other notions also persist despite the fact that neither is true. The first is that physical withdrawal is the heart of addiction. Addiction and physical dependence are considered to be the same thing, and so people believe that one is not addicted until he or she ends up with the shakes. The second notion, also false, is at the opposite end of the spectrum. It is the belief that addiction is psychogenic, in other words, that psychological forces are the ones which drive individuals to drink and drug until they end up needing drugs to keep from falling apart. And the corollary to this already mistaken notion is that the weakness of character which causes addiction also explains why addicts relapse after they have quit. The erroneous notion is that irresponsibility causes addiction, and weakness keeps addicts addicted. The notion is neat but just too simplistic.

Dual Forces: To think of addiction as purely psychological is a mistake. To think of it as purely biochemical is another mistake. Neither of those forces alone explains why rational human beings, some of whom exhibit commendable control in other areas of their lives, persist in using drugs even after it is clear that drugs are killing them.

If nothing else, becoming addicted is not simple. To persevere in using immoderate amounts of drugs, one must have a nervous system which permits such use, and a brain which responds in some special or unusual ways to drugs. An individual must also be able to tolerate high doses of drugs if he is to become addicted to them. He must get enough pleasure from drugs that the risk of using them seems worth it. Addiction is a complex matter.

Anyone who becomes sick, groggy or dizzy from drugs is not a likely candidate for a drug addiction. The person who falls asleep from a second drink is not very likely to have a third. But the body's response to drugs is not the only prerequisite for addiction. A person must also have the kind of mind which relishes the pleasure of drinking, enjoys the energizing effect of alcohol, and sees drinking as somehow appropriate to his lifestyle. To become addicted a person must be enough enamored of drugs so as to slip more readily into denying difficulties which result from using them. Without both the brain of an addict and the mind of one, a person either gets no kick from drugs or doesn't consider what he does get a big deal.

Though individuals with a family history of addiction appear more prone than others, research has not pinpointed precisely what makes one biochemically prone. The potential for addiction might some day be explained in terms of how readily a particular individual develops tolerance. It might be explained in terms of how certain individuals adapt to the stress potent toxins put on their brains. Addicts may be those people who find it necessary to use immoderate amounts of a drug to get the kick a drug has to offer. And if human beings behave like lab animals, research into tetrahydroisoquinolines (THIQ) might explain why those who produce high levels of acetaldehyde when drinking might drink in compulsive ways and become dependent on drugs, as appears the case with experimental animals injected with these THIQs (cf. Myers and Melchior, 1977). Some combination of these may explain why some become addicted while others do not.

How addicts differ from non-addicts and from each other also appears to differ with individual drugs. One person finds a particular drug a mellow experience, while another finds the same drug energizing. Both may be prone to the drug but for different reasons. Those who like the peace sedatives provide are more susceptible to sedatives than those who get groggy when using them. Obviously individuals who find stimulants energizing will be drawn to them more than those who find stimulants agitating.

Research is likely to conclude that there is no single path to addiction, but that a cluster of biochemical and psychological propensities explains why one person is prone and another protected. Again, it should be obvious that those who get great pleasure from drugs are more susceptible than those who do not. If the former tolerates high doses, his susceptibility increases, and the latter is protected from drug abuse both by his lack of response and his lack of tolerance. If one person experiences drinking as relaxing; another finds it stimulating, and a third enjoys both the "whee" and the "ah," all three will be susceptible, though the lure the drug holds for the third is twofold. And if that third person finds that by increasing the dose of the drug he increases its pleasure, and if he finds that he has no protective reaction against high doses, he will be saddled with several times the susceptibility of the others. Dr. Mark Schuckit in an article nearly everyone will understand summarizes the mechanisms which might well explain problem drinking (Schuckit, 1980a). The point is this. In order to become an addict one must have more than a mind to. He must have a nervous system susceptible to addiction, and this involves more than simply using too much of a drug for too long.

Still A Mystery: Addiction's exact cause or causes remain a mystery. We do not know yet whether those who are susceptible are born with the brain and the mind which are its ingredients, or whether they are born with its chemistry and develop its thinking only after exposure to drugs, or the reverse. We are not sure what precisely the ingredients of susceptibility happen to be. Definitions, therefore, tend to describe addiction rather than cite its causes. What we know about addiction is analogous to what we know about a magnetic field. It exists. It is powerful. It is predictable. It is describable. But what it is, we're not sure.

What Addiction Is Not: Addictive drug use is clarified by contrasting it to other ways of using drugs which are not in the nature of addiction. Drug taking may be described by any of the following words:

Drug Use—Nearly everyone has taken a prescription drug at some time or other. Many Americans drink alcohol, and more than a few use "recreational" drugs. "Use" describes drug taking which causes no harm, which causes no problems.

Drug Abuse—Drug abuse is drug taking which is harmful, risky or dangerous. Drug abuse is problematic, but it is not addiction. Not everyone who drinks too much once in a great while is rightly characterized an "abuser." Nor is everyone who abuses drugs automatically a drug addict.

Drug Reliance—To avoid the confusion about the word "dependence" which describes both a physical and a psychological condition, the word "reliance" is used here to describe those people who consistently count on drinking or drug taking to change how they feel. Unlike those who are not tolerant of drugs, do not lose control of them, and cause no harm to self or others when drinking, someone who counts on booze to change how he feels might be called alcohol **reliant**.

Drug Dependence—Dependence describes the physical state characterized by withdrawal when an individual abruptly stops using a drug. Dependence, in other words, is used here to mean physical dependence, not psychological dependence.

Addiction—Addiction is unusual involvement with a drug. It is not identical to physical dependence. Though addiction may include physical dependency, we need not wait until someone becomes dependent to call him an addict. An addict is that person who tries to control his drinking and/or drugging, but fails. Addicts differ from those who are drug reliant because both tolerance and loss of control characterize addictive use.

Dependence and Addiction: Most people make the mistake of thinking that addiction is physical dependence. It is an axiom of language that whenever two words describe exactly the same phenomenon, one of those words will eventually disappear from the living language. This has not yet happened to "addiction" and "dependence," and it is not likely to happen because there is a clear difference between them, a difference illustrated from hypothetical if not actual cases.

If a patient is given narcotics to relieve the pain of surgery, he will become dependent on narcotics administered long enough—a short time actually. The patient will be unable to stop taking the drug without going into withdrawal. But how should we describe this patient, if once he is withdrawn, he never seeks and never uses narcotics or any other drug again? Consider how different he is from the person who takes narcotics for the same reason, but who does pursue drugs and continues to use them after he has been taken off them. Both were physically dependent on narcotics at one time, but only one persisted in using narcotics. Does it make sense to call both "drug addicts?" It is unlikely that every soldier who was given morphine to relieve the pain of battle wounds returned to the States to become a junkie. Some did. Others did not. And it blurs the differences between them to consider both of them addicts just because they were both physically dependent at one point in their lives. Such use of language serves neither linguists nor health professionals.

The current *Diagnostic and Statistical Manual, DSM IV* defines Substance Dependence, the highest degree of the problem, without requiring physical withdrawal as part of that diagnosis. The conclusion one might infer is that physical dependence is not an addict's most serious problem, and it isn't. When viewed from the perspective of which is more serious, physical or psychological dependence, it becomes apparent that physical dependence is distressing and painful but is resolved in a short time with little psychic effort on the sufferer's part, whereas an addict's psychological drive may take years and a major effort to overcome.

Besides, addiction proves no less fatal without withdrawal. A nineteen-year-old had been found guilty of driving while intoxicated several times. His driver's license had been revoked. His tolerance was high. He attended AA meetings on and off for a year, and he acknowledged that he wanted to stop drinking.

One night he died while driving drunk. Though he never suffered withdrawal whenever he stopped drinking, his drive for alcohol—his addiction to it—proved no less fatal. Physical dependence complicates addiction, and that complication for some is serious indeed, but addiction is complicated enough even without the shakes.

Use and Addiction: Addiction is obviously not simply drug use, but an explanation of "use" helps to clarify addiction by contrast. Drugs are used in two ways: by prescription and as recreation - for health and for fun. Which drugs should be accepted as social or recreational, and which not, sparks heated debate in almost any gathering. One group accepts marijuana as recreational; another does not. Cocaine is considered dangerous today, whereas in the late 1980s some people considered it a form of recreational drug use (and some do still). The debate about which drugs ought to be considered socially acceptable is likely to persist, and yet debaters might agree on what constitutes social use even though they continue to disagree about to which drugs the criteria ought to apply.

Social-Recreational Use

Social drug use may be interpolated from social drinking, and social drinking differs from addictive drinking in several ways. Social drinkers use alcohol socially and sociably. They drink on social occasions and act in socially acceptable ways. Their drinking is moderate and limited. Most important of all, it causes no problems. It is not the social drinker's pattern to insult his brain with toxic doses. He is not stoned, sloshed, wasted, or smashed on a regular basis. For him intoxication is atypical. He may get drunk on a New Year's Eve, he may even intend to get drunk, but drunk is not his style. His pattern is to have a few drinks over several hours, feel mildly euphoric, have coffee, and go home. He does not arrive at parties half lit, gulp down several drinks, get loud and thick-tongued, belt down one for the road, and top the evening off with a nightcap before passing out.

Prescription Drug Use

A drug which is recommended by a licensed physician for a health purpose is what is called prescription use. The physician determines the drug's dose, frequency and route of administration, and only the physician prescribes changes in those directions. Prescription use is not meant to be harmful; the treating physician manages harmful side effects and stops the drug if necessary. Finally, a prescription drug is discontinued when health returns. Taking pills from a friend is not prescription use. To party with pills, to self prescribe, or to double the recommended dose is not legitimate prescription use. To save pills to be taken all at once is not using them as prescribed. And it can hardly be called legitimate prescription use to continue taking a drug fifteen years after one has regained his health.

Abuse and Addiction: The line between drug use and drug abuse is crossed when drug use causes problems. Drug abuse is quite simply any use that causes problems. The line that separates drug abuse from drug addiction is more difficult to draw. Although the criteria for drug abuse in the *Diagnostic Manuals (*both the *DSM III-R and DSM IV)* does include one's persistence in taking drugs despite recurrent problems caused by them, it is precisely that "persistence" which suggests a more serious problem than the word, "abuse," suggests. "Problems" distinguish use from abuse. What distinguishes abuse from addiction is "persistence" despite problems. Drinking enters a special realm when one keeps doing that which harms him. Abusers and addicts may drink equal amounts, but it is not the amount which makes one an addict. It is his persistence after he has lost job, family, self-respect and health which marks the difference between him and an abuser as qualitative. Prudence, common sense, reason, and will power do not have nearly as strong a grip on a person as does his drug.

Addictable Drugs: Are some drugs abusable and others not? Are some drugs merely abusable while others are addictable? Are there two separate categories for drugs? Only when the criteria for addiction requires evidence of measurable physical dependence will the list of addictable drugs differ from the list of abusable ones. Drugs have potential for abuse when they affect the brain in a way perceived as desirable or pleasurable, and such drugs generally fall into the category of mood altering drugs: depressants, stimulants, and hallucinogens. A drug is addictable if, besides producing pleasure, tolerance for the drug develops. Drugs capable of causing withdrawal may be addictable, but they are not addictable because of withdrawal. They are addictable because they are pleasurable, because tolerance for them develops, and because addicts feel "called" by them long after withdrawal. Is marijuana addictable? Only those who believe a drug must cause profound withdrawal, as is the case with alcohol, insist that marijuana is not addictable. Marijuana is pleasurable. Tolerance for it does, in fact, develop. And some of its users find marijuana nearly impossible to stop. For these reasons marijuana is as addictable as alcohol, opiates, stimulants, tranquilizers, cocaine, barbiturates and nicotine. In the drama of addiction the drug is but one member of the cast. The complete program includes a list of addiction prone people as well as a list of addictable drugs. Both lists are likely to prove complex.

Reliance and Addiction: By definition mood altering drugs alter moods, and though human beings are born with natural ways of changing the way they feel, people seem eager to find easier and quicker ways of doing anything. At some time or other a majority of Americans take a drink to relax. When alcohol or another drug consistently serves that purpose, such use becomes life limiting at the very least, and such a user might be called alcohol or drug reliant. If a person's drug use is not marked by tolerance, if it causes no problems, and if it is consistently under his or her control (he sets a modest limit and sticks to it), reliance might adequately describe someone who drinks to relax on a consistent basis. A tolerant drinker who loses control and who has problems because of drinking is best described by another word. His drug involvement is more complicated.

terature of chemical dependency "reliance" is not ...d to describe a form of drug taking, and the term might prove more useful in a hypothetical rather than statistical way, since the numbers of those who are drug reliant and not already abusers or addicts is probably quite small. There is also a risk that a word, such as "reliance," creates a category which addicts will seize on to describe their own use when it is obvious they are addicted. Nevertheless "reliance" may provide a useful way to describe a schizophrenic's drinking or pot smoking when that use aims at relieving psychotic symptoms. If the schizophrenic patient does not lose control, is not tolerant, and if his use causes no problems, then he might be described as "relying" on a drug.

Reliance might also describe a few teenagers (perhaps very few) who drink or smoke pot at parties as a way of dealing with shyness, self consciousness and inhibition, provided, of course, those teenagers are not tolerant, do not lose control, and have no recurrent problems due to drug use. In other words, teenagers who are not already drug abusers or drug addicts might be called alcohol or marijuana reliant, and in need of counseling because of it.

To rely on drugs as a way of dealing with life's stress is not healthy, and adults and young people alike would be well advised to find natural ways to alter their moods before relying on drugs to do so. But reliance on a drug is not addiction to a drug. The drive which pushes addicts goes far beyond their counting on drugs to change the way they feel. That drive is progressive, time-consuming, preoccupying, overwhelming, and increasingly obsessional. For addicts, drugs are not merely a means to reward success or relieve inhibition. They are central. Non-addicts can take it or leave it. Addicts nearly always claim they can, but they cannot.

Progressive Signs of Addiction: Severe addiction does not develop instantly, without warning. A series of signs foreshadows it, and those signs include:

- growing desire for the pleasure, joy or relief of drugs.

- willingness to experiment with improving the "high."
- willingness to spend increasing amounts of money for drugs.
- tendency to maximize the pleasure and minimize the pain of one's drug use.
- tendency for drinking / drug use to dominate conversation.
- growing tendency to rely on drugs for relief.
- neglect of past interests and hobbies.
- increasing value placed on paraphernalia.
- tendency to decline invitation where alcohol or other drugs will not be available.
- tendency to choose drinking over other recreational alternatives.
- forgetfulness of the interests, agenda and activities of family members.
- difficulty limiting drug use to appropriate times and places.
- self consciousness about use.
- perception that sober time is boring, and high time brief.
- tendency to hurry though one's routine to get to drinking.
- continued use though prudence, common sense and past experience indicate it is unsafe.
- tendency to choose companions and environments which mask use and intoxication.
- tendency to rearrange schedules to suit use.
- drifting toward a lifestyle which suits one's drug use.
- tendency to avoid non-users and gravitate to users.
- tendency to discount behavior under the influence.
- tendency to ridicule sober or "straight" people.
- tendency to associate drinking and drugging with even routine activities.
- tendency to sacrifice values, principles and ideals for the sake of the drug.

- preoccupation with past use and attempts to recapture it.
- growing preoccupation with the next use.
- deciding to end a personal relationship rather than stop using.
- growing need to justify frequency and / or amount.
- irritability with those who question use.
- drinking and drugging to feel normal.
- neglect of health, grooming and routine self-care.
- irritability when frustrated from use.
- continuing use after it has created or exacerbated health, job, family, school, and legal problems.
- neglect of family and responsibilities.
- anxiety while purchasing the drug.
- without drug use, pleasure becomes difficult.
- personal and family property sold to finance use.
- anxiety about running out.
- irritability and depression when not using.
- growing undefined fears and free floating anxiety.
- resigning oneself to reduced personal, moral, social and ethical standards because of use.
- tendency to take risks either to get drugs, or while under their influence.
- fear of insanity.
- inability to stop without help.

Addiction: An addict is an individual who is tolerant of drugs, who loses control of their use, who is unable to abstain or to limit his use after repeated attempts or despite a desire to do so, and who persists in using drugs despite problems caused by them. To qualify as an addict one need not suffer withdrawal. Tolerance and loss of control, however, are essential to the diagnosis. Tolerance and loss of control are problems all by themselves. In a hypothetical world, if one were to develop drug tolerance without manifesting any other sign of a drug problem, the tolerance itself would be a problem of some magnitude. The tolerant drinker has no choice but to drink in harmful amounts in order to get what drinking has to offer. To get high he must suffer harm. A tolerant alcoholic faces a dilemma not unlike the cancer patient who has become tolerant of painkillers. Painkillers may cause as much dysfunction as pain. And so, even if tolerance is not currently causing problems, tolerance can hardly keep from becoming a cause of future problems, at the very least, health problems. Tolerance, therefore, is a problem.

That loss of control is problematic is obvious. Someone who cannot predict how much he will drink, for how long, and what will happen as a result has an undeniable drinking problem. His drinking is unpredictable, and that is a problem.

Those who are tolerant or who lose control have built-in problems and should, therefore, have reason to stop. If they can stop, and if they can do so with ease, who is to say that they are addicted? For addicts, stopping is tough. They try but fail. They may for a time succeed, but eventually they pick up again. When an addict does manage to stop, it is often with a struggle—a psychic struggle. He cuts down, but eventually he goes back to and surpasses old levels. With strong motivation, under pressure, or with a stable external structure, alcoholics have quit drinking for periods of time, but sooner or later they pick up and are out of control again. An alcoholic who is strongly motivated might manage to drink without getting drunk for a time, but eventually he does get drunk, and it happens often at the worse time and with the worse results. That an alcoholic is never able to stop, that addictive drinking is one long and continuous affair, is a myth. The truth is that, before the final stage, most alcoholics can stop if they want to. Their problem is that they have little desire to do so, and when they do, it doesn't last long.

Addiction does not have a single face. Addiction may cause mild problems or severe ones. It may hit the mainstream of society or those in a counter-culture. An addiction may be riddled with illegal activity, or it may involve not a single illegal act. It may be longstanding or of recent onset. Cravings may be mild or intense. Addiction may be complicated by physical dependence with severe withdrawal symptoms, or it may be withdrawal-free. A motivating secondary gain, financial profit for instance, may keep one addict using longer than another one who gets only wasted from his addiction. There is, after all, more than one way to get loaded from addiction. Such considerations may help treatment teams determine the type of interventions appropriate for particular patients, but they are not addiction itself. Addiction happens to cigarette smokers and heroin mainliners, to drinkers and speed freaks, to cocaine snorters and prescription takers.

Cycles of Addiction: In *I'll Quit Tomorrow,* Vernon Johnson describes alcoholism as developing in phases, starting with a learning phase and ending in harmful dependency (Johnson, pp. 16-34). Addiction involves cycles. Drug use spawns itself. At the start of an addiction, drugs are used because they are pleasurable, because the drinker likes the high or because the prescription user likes the relief, and those are the motives for continuing. Later, drinking or drugging causes silly or outrageous behavior, and shame and guilt then join the addict's growing list of reasons for drinking. At some point that list includes drinking to solve problems. And finally addiction creates anxiety, resentment, bitterness and isolation, and those emotions become added reasons for drinking. Withdrawal is simply one more reason for continuing, and it reaches its peak when one drinks for little more than a reprieve from the terror drinking has created.

Eventually addiction needs no push from outside forces to keep going. Family members blame themselves for an addict's continued drinking, not realizing that their loved one will continue his use with or without them. Addiction survives divorce and separation. Eventually addiction generates all the force it needs to continue. It becomes autonomous, self-sustaining. It has a life of its own.

Drives and Cravings: Addicts know well what science has a difficult time proving, craving exists. Drug cravings occur during withdrawal, but they are not to be equated with withdrawal since cravings exist before one becomes physically dependent, and they continue long after he has withdrawn. Cravings are not provoked only by emotional distress; pleasurable associations trigger them too. Sometimes cravings come without any apparent stimulus. To attribute cravings exclusively to psychological pain is misleading. To ascribe them to pleasurable stimuli alone is equally misleading. Furthermore, because cravings are different with different drugs, it seems more reasonable to attribute them to physical processes than to psychological ones. Cigarette smokers describe craving for nicotine as quick pulse-like urges which come in prolonged and repeated waves. Alcoholics, sober for six months, describe alcohol craving as quick, viselike, lasting sometimes minutes and sometimes hours.

One reason craving is difficult to pinpoint is that careless use of language has clouded the issue. "Craving," "drive," and "urge," all have been used so interchangeably that determining whether they describe one or several different phenomena is nearly impossible. Addicts, however, know what cravings are, regardless of how confusing the language that describes them might be.

Non-addicts find it difficult to understand what drives addicts, and so that force is better understood through metaphors. The addictive drive is a desire for alcohol to fashion a world where life is serene, where snow is pure, and birds never cackle. Addiction's drive is a passion, an urge for a world where no imperfections exist—where the men are strong, the women good looking, and the children above average. Addicts respond in Pavlovian ways to certain events and to arrangements of people and places. A fragrance, a particular restaurant, and a well scrubbed home, even putting on a tuxedo, might trigger an urge to drink. For addicts, time distorts in a way similar to the way it distorts for a child at Christmas. Sober time seems as long as Christmas Eve, an eternity from the child's point of view; drinking time is like Christmas Day—over in a blink. The addictive urge is the unreachable itch in the middle of the back. It is magnetic, drawn to drinkers and drinking, druggers and drugging. A new addiction is a love affair, complete with the wonder, excitement and enchantment of it all. An old addiction is like a burnt out marriage or the debt on the car that is being towed away. No matter how painful past drug use has been, addicts believe that the next time drugs will deliver the power, joy, magic, clarity, excitement, and romance they used to.

If cravings paid attention to logic or fear, if cravings heeded negative reinforcement, then addicts who have lost jobs, families, self respect, and lungs because of nicotine and alcohol would not crave those drugs. But addiction is deaf to logic. It flies in the face of common sense.

As addiction progresses, it pushes drinking from pleasant diversion to center stage, displacing families, friends, hobbies, jobs, recreations, goals and self-respect. Though an addict denies it, his main preoccupation is his drug. He cherishes drugs. He loves them. What any individual values may be judged by where he spends his resources: his time, his money, and his mind. When drinking structures a chunk of one's time, when it spends most of his available money, chooses his friends, replaces his recreations, consumes his psychic energy, and plots his lifestyle, and risks his life for drugs, then the force which drives him is as powerful as any force we know—as powerful as the will to survive. When an alcoholic ends a marriage rather than stop drinking, it is drinking he loves. And addiction is a cruel lover.

10

The Family's Illness

Calling alcoholism a family illness could mean that alcoholism runs in families, and it does. It could mean that individuals may be born pre-disposed to developing an alcohol problem, and this is also true. However, what is meant most often by calling addiction a family illness is that those who live with alcoholics and other addicts get sick too, as sick emotionally as alcoholics themselves, sometimes even sicker. From the beginning Alcoholics Anonymous recognized that to a certain extent "the entire family of an alcoholic is ill" (Alcoholics Anonymous, p. 122). For family members who never drank, this is hard to take. Having put up with active alcoholism, one is hardly flattered to be called sick and in need of help at the start of recovery.

The Mathematics of a Family's Illness: Getting sick from living with alcoholism is practically unavoidable. The forces at work on individuals are multiple and powerful, and when added together, their impact is considerable. To escape the experience unaffected would be miraculous.

To live with an alcoholic is to live with his symptoms and to do so for a long time. It is to live with denial, guilt, anger, fear, shame, and sadness. To trust an alcoholic is to trust someone whose thinking is drug distorted. To help an addict is to find that one's best efforts have little or no effect, and at times seem to make matters worse. It is confusing and frustrating to say the least.

Living with Symptoms: A person dying from a terminal illness, such as cancer, feels some very powerful emotions—sadness, anger and fears. Living with these feelings has an effect on members of their family. The family who lives with one who suffers from a degenerative mental illness lives with strange behaviors as well, and that behavior affects the family. The family of an alcoholic lives with both; it is a disease which is capable of killing its victim at any moment, and it is an illness which produces disturbing behavioral and psychological symptoms. The impact is predictable.

The range and intensity of an alcoholic's symptoms is phenomenal. He is drunk, moody, unpredictable, suicidal, manipulative, rageful, resentful, ashamed, guilty, fearful and terrified. He is as suddenly explosive as he is unexpectedly gentle. He may be abusive physically and emotionally. His love and his neglect are equally unpredictable. An alcoholic's family is exposed to nearly every symptom in the psychiatric textbooks in addition to an addict's physical health problems. When addicts are drug-poisoned or in withdrawal, family members witness psychotic behavior, delusions, hallucinations and paranoia.

The Impact of a Long History: The family of a cancer patient may live with the emotional pain of that problem for several years, but alcoholic families live with alcoholism for ten, twenty, thirty or more years, and do so without knowing that they are living with a disease. Not only is stress cumulative, the insidiousness of chemical dependency is that families live with its pathology for so long that pathology seems the normal state of affairs. And in more than a few cases the person who is supposed to be sick looks quite well, and at times is even accorded respect from the world in which he works.

It is common for children of alcoholics to grow up accepting unusual and bizarre behavior as if it were normal. A teenager whose father had an enormous tolerance for booze was sixteen years old before he realized that most men cannot drink a fifth of whiskey in an evening and hold a coherent conversation. His father could. Addicts and alcoholics are famous for "crashing." In such homes, children awaken to find strangers sprawled all over the living room floor asleep, their home regularly invaded by a father's or brother's or sister's or mother's drinking buddies. These children grow up with little privacy and less sense of their right to it. They live in homes without boundaries. And if the alcoholic parent is magnanimous and the non-addicted parent nasty and vindictive, their confusion multiplies. There is more.

Living with Denial and Blame: Cancer patients do not blame their loved ones for causing the disease. Alcoholics do blame others, and family members come in for a major share of that blame. An addict's denial affects his or her family members, causing them to doubt their perceptions and their ability to interpret events occurring around them. It erodes their self-confidence and self esteem. Either directly or by innuendo, the addict's message to his family is that they are at fault. If they were somehow different, he would not be as he is and do what he does. An alcoholic's spouse may have been told many times that if she "were a better wife, more affectionate, sexier, a better lover, cook, provider, or companion," things would be different, and he would not look for companionship elsewhere. Alcoholics have accused their spouses of being cold, cruel, stupid, ugly, insensitive, phony and unloving. Anyone who is told repeatedly that he is stupid is affected by the criticism, and the damage doubles when it comes from a trusted source. A spouse thinks, "No one is closer to me. I have trusted him with my deepest thoughts. I can't ignore his opinion." This makes people sick, but there is more.

Living with Guilt: Alcoholism assaults self-esteem on several fronts. For the family that does not accept chemical dependency as a disease, family members are easily persuaded that they have caused it and quite naturally feel guilty about that. Family members judge themselves as cruel, incompetent, worthless, vicious and powerful, all at the same time. But family guilt and shame result not only from an addict's accusations toward them. An extra helping of those feelings result from their own rage, bitterness, hatred, and even murderous feelings. Finally, it is impossible to maintain self-esteem if you feel not only that you have caused a problem but also that you are powerless to do anything about it, and that feeling is common for alcoholic families. Each time the family fails to get its alcoholic loved one sober, members feel powerless and impotent—and even more determined to try harder next time. There is more.

Living with Anger: Frustration, hurt, broken trust and miscommunication are common triggers for anger. If so, living with alcoholics provides ample opportunities for anger. It does not, however, provide healthy models for dealing with anger. One of alcoholism's many ironies is that family members learn to deal with their anger in the same way addicts deal with theirs, either by stuffing it or blowing it.

There is little wonder why the husband or wife or children of an addict stuff their anger. They have good reasons to. A child who is told repeatedly that he is stupid by someone whose judgment he trusts begins to believe it. To express anger, however, one must believe he has rights. In fact, anger is at times just that, an expression of one's rights. But family members who believe they are stupid or guilty or incompetent, quite naturally presume that they have no right to be angry. "Who am I to find fault with others?" And so, anger is either stuffed or denied. Even when a family member believes his anger is justified, he or she is still afraid to express it because the price, emotional isolation, abuse or abandonment, is too high. But there is more.

Living with Fear: Alcoholic families live with fear, the triple fears of abuse, abandonment and death. The impact is far reaching. The elderly parents of a young marijuana addict would regularly awaken in the middle of the night to see if the gas stove had been left on because their son's habit was to come home late, fix something to eat and forget to turn off the stove. More than once they found the downstairs filled with smoke. And if the phone rang when their son was out, fear immobilized them, never sure what the call might mean. There is more.

Enabling and Its Frustrations: Enablers serve addicts in several ways. They rescue them from jams. They help them deny their addiction. They cover up its consequences. If they nag, they provide drinkers and druggers with excuses for drinking and drugging.

Enabling is not an act of stupidity or cruelty. It is motivated by understandable emotions: fear, guilt, love and hope. Family members enable because they are afraid of what will happen if they do not. They enable because they hope enabling will work, that somehow it will help. They enable because they think they owe it—out of loyalty. They cover up for an alcoholic's drunken behavior to avoid its shame. They enable because they believe enabling shows they care. Occasionally an individual family member enables because he or she benefits from enabling. In a family with two alcoholics, one will enable the other in order to keep the focus off himself—to hide behind another's problem. A parent who gets the respect of his or her children because he or she is long-suffering, noble and self-sacrificing finds it difficult to stop enabling and give up the admiration which comes as a result of it.

Family members do not regard enabling as helping addiction continue. They believe they are trying to get it to stop. They think that by rescuing they will stir up enough gratitude in an alcoholic for him to want to stop drinking, that by making excuses for him he will return the favor and act responsibly, that by nagging they will wear him down, and he'll change. And when their efforts have little or no effect, or when their enabling makes matters worse, families are frustrated and frightened and all the more desperate to control. Enabling is exhausting. But there is more.

Responsibility without Control: Those who live with someone who is out of control will almost instinctively respond by taking control or trying to. Family members assume responsibility for all sorts of things, for keeping an alcoholic in a good mood, for managing his drunkenness, for scheduling social life around him, for taking care of the household, for managing the atmosphere so as not to provoke drinking or drugging. Family members assume responsibility for explaining an alcoholic's behavior to others, for protecting others from his abuse, and for preventing fatal consequences when he is drunk. Individual members assume responsibility for entire families, reasoning that if someone doesn't take charge, disaster is sure to follow. The problem is that all the while a family member strives for control, he or she realizes at some level that he has neither the power nor the means to control. A knot in one's stomach is so often the result when people feel both responsible and powerless, and that knot doesn't go away until one learns what Al-Anon calls "letting go."

"Sometimes Sicker": At treatment facilities it is the custom to introduce new patients and accompanying family members to the staff members who are on duty at the time of admission. At one facility on one such occasion, one staff member missed the introductions, and when he finally met the couple was astonished at how weakened and exhausted the man was, certain that his withdrawal would be difficult and that it would be days before this poor chap would recover from the beating alcoholism had given him. The staff member had made one mistake. The man was not the patient. His wife was. Her husband was exhausted from the tasks of living with an addict. In another instance, a woman accompanied her husband the morning of his admission, a day on which she had scheduled a business appointment for herself later that afternoon. During the admitting process, she managed a smile and a business-like manner until her husband was taken off for his physical examination. No sooner had he left the room then she turned to the staff and said, "I hope someone here finally gives it to that son-of-a-bitch." With that she marched down the hall, then stopped and turned around. With tears streaming down her face, she said to the staff member who had followed her, "Please apologize to those people for me. I'm sorry. I just don't know what I feel anymore."

Al-Anon and Nar-Anon: Families who fail to get help for themselves remain governed by confusing emotions and motivations, often unconsciously so. Reading books and attending lectures about addiction helps, but insight is usually not enough. Minds need information, that is certain, but pain is at another level, and it is feeling which must heal. Family recovery is the goal of Al-Anon and Nar-Anon, organizations that have helped many. These groups are most helpful, however, when one goes to them for the right person and for the right reason. Alcoholics do not recover because their families attend Al-Anon meetings. Addicts do not stop using drugs because their parents go to Nar-Anon. It is the family which gets well at Al-Anon and Nar-Anon. The husband of an alcoholic makes his first mistake if he thinks Al-Anon will teach him how to get his wife sober. He makes his second mistake if he believes that his own emotional well-being depends on her recovering.

Recovery for a family commences when its members accept that they have something to recover from. The axiom of recovery is as true for the family as it is for the alcoholic—in order to get well, one must first be sick. The toughest part about getting well is admitting you need to.

Al-Anon can be helpful in two situations, living with an active alcoholic and living with a recovering one. Some Al-Anon members wonder which of those situations is more difficult.

Coping with An Active Addict: Living with addiction is frustrating, frightening, painful and disturbing. It is not, however, impossible. Family members are living with surprising equanimity because they have learned a few of the principles that guide self help groups.

There is, of course, no foolproof recipe for getting an alcoholic sober. There are "Do's" and "Don'ts" which might persuade an alcoholic to enter treatment and at the same time provide some peace of mind for his family.

Do	**Don't**
Detach	**Ask Why**
Live Life	**Bluff**
Concentrate on Self	**Enable**
Confront with Love	**Be The Cure**

Detach

To survive in an alcoholic environment a family must learn not to blame itself for causing the alcoholic's disease or for creating the behavior it produces. Al-Anon members learn three **C**s: "you can't *Cause* it; you can't *Control* it, and you can't *Cure* it." Detachment means internalizing those three **Cs.**

Detachment does not mean sitting silently by and watching a loved one get sicker and sicker until he hits bottom. It does not mean that someone is supposed to stop loving and stop caring. It does mean that one can let go of the illusion that he is in control of another person, and quite surprisingly—that is all one lets go of, an illusion. Detachment means that one understands that addiction progresses at the direction of a disease, and that family members, no matter how powerful they may be, cannot cause that disease; they cannot cause another person's nervous system to tolerate drugs. A woman may be as mean as the "Wicked Witch of the West," but no act of hers can alter her husband's brain and liver function. Detachment means accepting this.

Detachment means that though one may take heroic measures to protect another from fatal consequences, he cannot control the course of a loved one's addiction; he cannot stop its progression, and he cannot prevent absolutely its consequences.

Detachment means that family members can learn they are not responsible for causing an addict's moods or for resolving them, a difficult lesson in a world with songs which encourage us to "make someone happy."

Somehow people have accepted the notion that love is demonstrated by simultaneous suffering, that if you really love someone who is in turmoil you too will be in turmoil. It is a notion which alcoholic families need to eschew. Detachment requires that family members learn not to wallow in self-pity because someone else wallows in it, nor thrash about agitated just because someone else is agitated and thrashes about. Because an alcoholic is in turmoil does not mean his family has to be in turmoil too. An addict will never learn that his drug use is compulsive and his behavior drug-affected if his family helps him delude himself into thinking that the family has the problem, that the problem is communal, caused by the group and shared in the same way by all its members. Difficult though it may be, a family may have to let the alcoholic suffer the pain of his disease alone, while his family gets on with life and enjoys as much as difficult circumstances permit.

Detachment is alien to those who believe that power is control. It is strange to those who think that winning demands fighting. Detachment is foreign and seems at first uncaring and unloving. Sustaining it without support from others is difficult. For this reason families find Al-Anon helpful.

Live Life

Families who make the alcoholic the center of their lives become prisoners. Regardless of how much an addict may want to control the mood at home, his family must avoid sitting around the house silent and moody. A family can enjoy a social life without flaunting it, which would be provocative and enabling, or without making excuses for it. Maintaining that balance takes effort, but it's possible. Spouses are advised to have friends of their own, pursue a job or career, and enjoy hobbies and recreation. Gaining personal autonomy helps prevent one from becoming trapped into enabling out of fear of being abandoned.

Concentrate on Self

To concentrate on changing an alcoholic's behavior is a waste of time. It doesn't work. It can't. To expect someone who is sick to act in a responsible, caring, loving, predictable, mature, attentive and even-tempered way—to ask a sick person to be less resentful, depressed, bitter, cynical and preoccupied—is doomed to fail. Symptoms do not disappear until one treats the disease which causes them. Family members are better off managing their own emotions, dealing with their own frustrations, handling their own fears, asserting their own needs, in short, concentrating on what they can control rather than spending energy on what they cannot control.

One truth, which takes a long time to learn and needs reinforcing on a regular basis, is that I *control* only myself, my own actions. When I try to control others, they resent it and resist it. I can guide, advise, counsel, urge, encourage, exhort, love, warn, set limits, and even enforce consequences, but I cannot control others. "The knot" goes away only when I accept this.

Confront with Love

If a family decides to wait for an alcoholic to hit bottom, they might have a very long wait, and a risky one. To expect someone with a drugged brain and a denying mind to gain insight, overcome denial, stop drinking, and change his ways is to hope for a quartet of miracles.

"Letting go" does not mean remaining mute. New Al-Anon members are advised to "shut up and smile" when things get hot, advice which is intended to help them avoid useless shouting matches, especially when a drunk is drunk. The advice does not mean that a member of the family should never open his or her mouth. Such silence may prove deadly.

Family members can learn to confront without anger and without malice. In Alcoholics Anonymous and in Al-Anon it is called "tough love." Both ingredients are essential. All love and no tough is as impotent as all tough and no love is provocative. Neither works by itself. Together they have power.

Denial is confronted by specific facts and truthful information. Generalities, such as "you drink too much," or "you are a mess when you're drunk," are ineffective; in fact, they are counterproductive. Confrontation does not mean yelling into another's face. Confrontation is the process by which one places the truth before another's eyes in a way that makes seeing it unavoidable and compelling. Confrontation simply means telling the truth lovingly, forcefully, concretely and specifically.

A wife confronts with love when she says something as direct and specific as,

> "What I want to say is difficult because I have been hurt and because I care enough not to hurt you. Last week you were drinking and called me a bitch. I was shocked and hurt. I know you are not the kind of person to say such things when you are not drinking. It scares me to see how you change when you drink. You never use language like that when you're not drinking."

To confront in a loving and specific way is to say, for example,

> "You are a smart, responsible person and a good friend. That's why it frightens me to see how drinking affects your memory. Last Friday you agreed to play tennis on Saturday morning, but you had six drinks, and when I called Saturday, you didn't remember the arrangements at all."

A teen-age daughter confronts her mother who has passed out at 7:00 p.m. when she phrases the confrontation this way,

> "You promised we would watch the late movie together. By six o'clock you had finished your eighth beer and were asleep. This is the second time this month that has happened. When you drink, you can't keep your promises (and if it is true, adds), I know you are a person who takes promises seriously."

If an alcoholic responds to such confrontations by picking a fight, family members should try to avoid fighting either by repeating their words or by withdrawing from the encounter in a manner which will not provoke anger. Sometimes it's not easy.

> "I'm trying to tell you I care enough to help you see how you change when you drink, and how it scares me. I'm not here to fight. I don't want to argue. I want you to know what I see."

These or similar words might avoid a fight which, if it happens, is likely to provide the addict an excuse to indulge. At times, no matter what one does, alcoholics will erupt in anger, and family members respond in kind. After all, alcoholics are sick.

Family Intervention: Confrontations of the sort mentioned above happen every day in alcoholic homes. The situation can, however, become so troubled and so thick with denial that a more structured intervention is necessary. Family Intervention is a process by which family members learn how to confront an addicted loved one, encourage him to enter treatment, and inform him of the consequences if he refuses. The process is planned, even rehearsed. It cannot be rushed. It is a tool best used as part of a plan and not in a moment of crisis, and it is best directed by a professional willing to spend the time it takes for a family to prepare themselves emotionally. Because intervention requires family members to confront out of love, families need time to get in touch with those feelings, often buried under layers of anger and fear. It is scary, and it involves risk.

It is unrealistic to expect someone in a family to resolve all of his anger before confronting. Nevertheless each member must be able to put his or her anger on hold long enough to confront without letting anger get in the way. And if a particular member cannot do this, he or she should either withdraw from the intervention, or the intervention should be delayed until they can keep their anger in check. Angry interventions prove to be enabling acts, not helpful ones.

Don't Ask Why

Knowing what causes alcoholism doesn't cure it. Knowing why someone drinks doesn't get it to stop. It is fruitless to ask,

"Why?" "Why me?" Even if such questions were answerable, the answers would not change the facts. It is more productive to figure out how to confront an alcoholic and how to intervene in the disease as early as possible rather than to ask why he got sick in the first place.

Don't Bluff

A person should deliver an ultimatum only if and when he or she is ready, willing and able to carry it out. Don't bluff! Before delivering an "or else," a family member must think through the consequences of the ultimatum and how to deal with them. The family member must be prepared to deal with the addict's response. And they must be capable of carrying out the ultimatum. A spouse who threatens to leave her husband but has no place to go delivers an idle threat, and idle threats are enabling. Talking the matter over with a counselor is recommended.

Don't Enable

An exhausted family which has energy for one thing and one thing only should use that energy figuring out how it enables an addict, and stop it. Sometimes alcoholics are helped not by what others do, but by what they stop doing. Stop rescuing. Stop nagging. Stop covering up. A family which provides financial support to an addict might consider cutting off the funds which support the addiction. One mother decided to buy groceries for her addicted son rather than give him the money to buy them because the money never went for groceries. If a spouse has in the past called work to make an excuse for an alcoholic's absence, the spouse should let the alcoholic make the call for himself. Someone who nags in an effort to get an alcoholic to stop drinking should stop nagging and force the alcoholic to find another excuse to drink besides the nagging—give him the chance to see his compulsion. If someone is tempted to bail an alcoholic out of jail, let him stay. Those who clean up his mess should leave the mess; let him clean it up. An addict will not deal with his addiction until he has to deal with its consequences, and a family which cleans up his mess helps him avoid that. The message is this. If you intend to swing on addiction's trapeze, you must know the nets are down.

Don't be the Cure

Families who treat addictive disease with only their own resources, believing that good books, vacations, a return to church, love and chicken soup are the cure, prolong the active disease and its relapses. Addiction and its denial are so complex that one wonders how anyone got sober in the old days when alcoholics were left with both depleted resources and wits. This is not the case today. Professionals treat addiction. Alcoholics Anonymous and Narcotic Anonymous work. When an alcoholic is ready for treatment, the family's job is to get him to treatment and then get help for themselves.

Initially addicts and families recover together by recovering individually, each member participating, each cooperating, each autonomous, and each attending his or her own meetings. It is not a good idea for recovering alcoholics and their spouses to attend the same self-help meetings all the time. They inhibit each other. One listens for the other instead of for himself.

Alcoholics do recover without supportive families. Families can recover while alcoholics drink. The ideal is for both to recover together, but sadly this is not always the case.

Ending a Relationship? There are times when continuing to live with an active alcoholic is destructive and is neither in the best interest of the addict's recovery nor his family's well being. Families are forced to consider whether to end a relationship.

Ending a relationship prematurely may be counter-productive, of course. To sever ties before a family has made at least several attempts to encourage a loved one to enter treatment succeeds only in creating guilt in family members and resentment in addicts. A family loses its self-respect if it makes no such efforts.

It is not easy to determine when to end a relationship, and it is unquestionably better to seek counsel in the matter than to let the decision be made by rage or by default. But when continuing a relationship is one of the very factors which enables an addiction to continue, then ending that relationship may be necessary, and families ought to seek help with the decision.

Coping with Recovery: Some relationships survive active addiction and get a shot at surviving early recovery, a trying time of unraveling knots, of resolving old feelings and dealing with new ones, of learning to live with uncertainty, of coming to grips with the problems recovery itself creates.

In early recovery families fear those changes which might occur when someone gets sober. They wonder if they will like him sober—much less love him. They wonder if he will love them. They fear relapse, or they expect it, especially if it has occurred repeatedly. They might have even become resigned to its inevitability.

Unfortunately, "forgive and forget" is a common idiom in our culture. To forgive is a formidable enough task, and for the family who believes that forgetting is essential to forgiving, the task may be impossible. The truth is that one might have to learn to forgive even though he may always remember.

Some families long to return to normal and are shocked when they realize that they have never been "normal," that alcoholism has been with them as long as they have been a family. Recovery is discovery rather than rediscovery for some.

All too often a family has a mess to clean up. If parents have been conflicted and contradictory about their discipline, children are resentful when parents agree and support each other. Leftover debts may have to be paid; a job may have to be found; legal problems may need to be resolved; a house may need repair.

A family member who has become accustomed to controlling an alcoholic's moods may not stop immediately. The energy one spends trying to control an alcoholic who is actively drinking is easily transferred into manipulating his recovery, coaxing him to attend the right AA meetings, to find the right sponsor, to work an honest program, participate in group therapy, or to take Antabuse. Family members walk on eggs for a while, feeling that they have to navigate around stressful issues in order to prevent relapse. It's not easy to let go of another's recovery and concentrate on one's own.

Accepting alcoholism as a disease that makes all members of a family sick, whose treatment is life-long abstinence, and whose recovery means changes in lifestyle and friendships is no small task.

Mistrust learned from years of hurt and broken promises takes time to rebuild. Trust is regained only through consistency repeated over time. It isn't easy, and it doesn't happen immediately. Trust cannot be forced, and it cannot be faked. It can, however, be relearned even when one is unable to forget the past.

When alcoholism has taught a family how to communicate in silent, indirect, passive or angry ways, learning to communicate directly is unfamiliar, awkward and uncomfortable at first.

Perhaps the most difficult task for a recovering family concerns recognizing and dealing with feelings—old feelings as well as new ones, new fears and new anger as well as new love and new trust.

The tasks seem formidable. They are. But recovery is not a fantasy. This very day recovery is a fact for millions.

References

Alcoholics Anonymous. 1976. Alcoholics Anonymous. (Third Edition) New York: Alcoholics Anonymous World Services, Inc.

American Medical Association. 1968. Manual on Alcoholism. Chicago: AMA.

American Psychiatric Association. 1987. Diagnostic and Statistical Manual of Mental Disorder DSM-III-R. Washington, D.C.: American Psychiatric Association.

American Society of Addiction Medicine and the National Council on Alcoholism and Drug Dependence, Inc. Joint Committee to Study the Definition and Criteria for the Diagnosis of Alcoholism, 4/26/90. 1990. NCADD Fact Sheet: Alcoholism and Alcohol-Related Problems." New York: National Council on Alcoholism and Drug Dependence, Inc.

Begleiter, H., B. Porjesz, B. Bihari, and B. Kissin. 1984. "Event-Related Brain Potentials in Boys at Rish for Alcoholism." Science 225:1493-1496.

Blasinsky, M., and G.K. Russell, eds. 1981. Urine Testing for Marijuana Use: Implications for a Variety of Settings. New York: The American Council for Marijuana and Other Psychoactive Drugs, Inc.

Cadoret, Remi J., E. Troughton, T.W. O'Gorman, and E. Heywood. 1986. "An Adoption Study of Genetic and Environmental Factors in Drug Abuse." Archives of General Psychiatry 43:1131-1136.

Cadoret, R.J., C.A. Cain, and W.M. Grove. 1980. "Development of Alcoholism in Adoptees Raised Apart from Alcoholic Biologic Relatives." Archives of General Psychiatry 37:561-563.

Cloninger, C.R. 1987. "Neurogenetic Adaptive Mechanisms in Alcoholism." Science 236:410-416.

_______. 1988. "Etiologic Factors in Substance Abuse: An Adoption Study Perspective," In Biological Vulnerability to Drug Abuse, ed. R.W. Pickens and D.F. Svikis. National Institute on Drug Abuse Research Monograph 89. Rockville Md.: DHHS Pub. No. (ADM) 88-1590.

Drews, Toby. 1983. Getting Them Sober, Volume 3. New Jersey: Bridge Publishing Inc.

Edwards, G., M. Gross, M. Keller, J. Moser, and R. Room. 1977. Alcohol-Related Disabilities. Geneva: World Health Organization.

Goodwin, Donald W. 1976. Is Alcoholism Hereditary? New York: Oxford University Press.

Goodwin, D.W. 1979. "Alcoholism and Heredity." Archives of General Psychiatry 36:57-61.

Goodwin, D.W., F. Schulsinger, L. Hermansen, S. B. Guze, and G. Winokur. 1973. "Alcohol Problems in Adoptees Raised Apart from their Alcoholic Biologic Parents." Archives of General Psychiatry 28:238-243.

Goodwin, D.W., F. Schulsinger, N. Moller, L. Hermansen, G. Winokur, and S. B. Guze. 1974. "Drinking Problems in Adopted and Nonadopted Sons of Alcoholics." Archives of General Psychiatry 31:164-169.

Jellinek, E.M. 1960. The Disease Concept of Alcoholism. New Haven, Connecticut: Hillhouse Press.

Johnson, Vernon. 1973. I'll Quit Tomorrow. New York: Harper & Row.

Keller, M., M. McCormick, and V. Efron. 1982. A Dictionary of Words about Alcohol. (Second Edition) New Brunswick, N.J.: Rutgers Center of Alcohol Studies.

Korsten, M.A., S. Matsuzaki, L. Feinman, and C.S. Lieber. 1975. "High Blood Acetaldehyde Levels after Ethanol Administration: Difference Between Alcoholic and Nonalcoholic Subjects." New England Journal of Medicine 292:386-389.

Kubler-Ross, Elisabeth. 1975. Death: The Final Stage of Growth. Englewood Cliffs: Prentice-Hall, Inc.

Lieber, C.S. 1976. "The Metabolism of Alcohol." Scientific American 234:25-33.

Milam, James, and Katherine Ketcham. 1981. Under The Influence: A Guide to the Myths and Realities of Alcoholism. Seattle: Madrona Publishers.

Myers, R.D., and C.L. Melchior. 1977. "Alcohol Drinking: Abnormal Intake Caused by Tetrahydropapaveroline in Brain." Science 196:554-556.

National Council on Alcoholism. 1976. "Definition of Alcoholism." Annals of Internal Medicine 85:764.

Pendery, M.L., I.M. Maltzman, and L.J. West. 1982. "Controlled Drinking by Alcoholics? New Findings and a Reevaluation of a Major Affirmative Study." Science 217:169-175.

Pollock, V.E., J. Volavka, D.W. Goodwin, S.A. Mednick, W.F. Gabrielli, J. Knop, and F. Schulsinger. 1983. "The EEG After Alcohol Administration in Men at Risk for Alcoholism." Archives of General Psychiatry 40:857-861.

Schuckit, M.A. 1980. "Alcoholism and Genetics: Possible Biological Mediators." Biological Psychicatry 15:437-447.

Schuckit, M.A. 1984a. Drug and Alcohol Abuse. New York: Plenum Press.

_______. 1984b. "Subjective Response to Alcohol in Sons of Alcoholics and Control Subjects." Archives of General Psychiatry 41:879-884.

Schuckit, M.A., D. Engstrom, R. Alpert, and J. Duby. 1981. "Differences in Muscle-Tension Response to Ethanol in Young Men with and without Family Histories of Alcoholism." Journal of Studies on Alcohol 42:918-924.

Schuckit, M.A., D.W. Goodwin, and G. Winokur. 1972. "A Study of Alcoholism in Half Siblings." American Journal of Psychiatry 128:1132.

Schuckit, M.A., and V. Rayses. 1979. "Ethanol Ingestion: Differences in Blood Acetaldehyde Concentrations in Relatives of Alcoholics and Controls." Science 203:54-55.

Sobell, M.B., and L.C. Sobell. 1973. "Alcoholics Treated by Individualized Behavior Therapy: One Year Treatment Outcome." Behavior Research and Therapy 11:599-618.

_______. 1976. "Second Year Treatment Outcome of Alcoholics Treated by Individualized Behavior Therapy: Results." Behavior Research and Therapy 14:195-215.

_______. 1978. Behavioral Treatment of Alcohol Problems. New York: Plenum Press.

Vaillant, George. 1983. The Natural History of Alcoholism: Causes, Patterns, and Paths to Recovery. Cambridge, Mass: Harvard University Press.

Wallgren, Henrik and Herbert Barry, III. 1970. Actions of Alcohol. Amsterdam: Elsevier Publishing Co., Inc.

Wegscheider, Sharon. 1981. Another Chance: Hope and Health for the Alcoholic Family. Palo Alto, CA: Science and Behavior Books, Inc.

Whitfield, Charles L. and Kenneth Williams. 1976. The Patient with Alcoholism and Other Drug Problems. 4th edition.

EPILOGUE

An alcoholic doesn't have a drinking problem. His is a "drunking" problem. In other words, the reason an alcoholic picks up a drink is not nearly as important as why he has trouble putting it down. This particular problem is properly called a disease, a destructive process that defies even heroic efforts at will power to manage it. Believing addiction is a disease is not easy. It is hampered by dozens of myths and misconceptions.

Several longstanding myths cloud our understanding of alcoholism and other drug addictions. That alcohol is truth serum is one. Alcohol is a serious, sedative drug. That alcoholics are bad or weak or irresponsible is another myth. A list of our nation's finest will include alcoholic actors, athletes, astronauts, and senators. That alcoholism is a moral problem or a symptom of a psychiatric disorder is another misconception, still widely believed. Alcoholism, a drug addiction, is a primary disease. No other name explains why good people with integrity and will power get caught in its grip and head toward incarceration, insanity or death.

Another misconception is that an "alcoholic personality" is the primary cause of alcoholism, and that myth persists even more than twenty years after Dr. George Vaillant's long-range study concluded that the alcoholic personality is not the cause of alcoholism, but its result. Addiction does change personality, and that change is, at times, profound. The term, personality of addiction, better captures the impact that long-term drug use has on an addict's brain, his mind, his feelings, and his spirit.

The axiom of recovery from addiction holds that no one recovers from a disease he or she does not have. Denial is the most serious barrier to recovery, and often requires professional help to overcome it. The other major barrier is hopelessness. Fortunately, for nearly seventy years Alcoholics Anonymous has held out the hope of recovery for those seeking help.

A disease produces symptoms, and drug addiction produces a list of symptoms of varying kinds: nervous system signs, social consequences, health, psychological, and behavioral problems. Tolerance, loss of control, and persistence despite recurrent problems caused by alcohol and other drugs indicate a serious problem with alcohol. But addiction does not simply produce symptoms in isolation from each other, those symptoms occur in a history, one symptom producing the conditions for another symptom, linked together in a dynamic chain of symptoms which is both progressive and predictable. That predictability, despite the variety of personalities to whom it occurs, is compelling evidence for thinking of addiction as a disease.

A third barrier to recovery for drug addicts (and this includes alcoholics) is that the disease is coupled with an early recovery period, which is distressing, painful and emotionally wrenching for both addicts and their families. A family member, already affected by the active disease, and sometimes quite seriously so, deals in early recovery with his own confusing feelings as well as the raw nervous system of someone newly sober. In early recovery, many are convinced that this disease intends to kill them. But recovery is not hopeless. Recovery happens every day.

About the Author

Since 1979, Dick Prodey has presented a series of lectures each week on Alcoholism and Chemical Dependency to audiences of addicts, their families and to health professionals at The Sheppard and Enoch Pratt Hospital in Towson, Maryland. These lectures, sponsored jointly by the Maryland Chapter of the National Council of Alcoholism and Drug Dependence and by Partners in Recovery, the addiction treatment program of The Sheppard and Enoch Pratt and The Greater Baltimore Medical Center hospitals, form the core of this book.

From 1980 to 1986, Mr. Prodey worked as Coordinator of the Alcoholism Program of The Sheppard and Enoch Pratt Hospital where he was responsible for the education and treatment of alcoholics, other drug addicts and their families. For more than twenty years, he has provided consultant and educational services to high schools, colleges and addictions treatment facilities in the greater Baltimore area. He has lectured on addiction and recovery to lay and professional audiences at hospitals, businesses and health-care facilities across the United States.

Mr. Prodey holds Masters degrees in Education and in Guidance and Counseling. He teaches courses on substance abuse in the Graduate Division of Loyola College in Maryland. He is a member of the board of The National Council of Alcoholism and Drug Dependence, Maryland Chapter, and is an advisor to The Getting Them Sober Foundation.

Today, Dick Prodey serves as the Director of Guidance and Counseling at Loyola Blakefield, a Jesuit preparatory school in Towson, Maryland. He lives with his wife, Pam, in Eldersburg, Maryland. His wife and three of his five children have also worked in counseling alcoholics, other addicts and their families.